THUNDERBIRDS
ARE GO!

ARE GO!

John Marriott

with a foreword by Gerry Anderson

ITC
Entertainment Group

B🌿XTREE

First published 1992 by
Boxtree Limited
36 Tavistock Street
London WC2E 7PB

© 1992 ITC Entertainment Group Ltd
Licensed by Copyright Promotions Ltd

3 5 7 9 10 8 6 4 2

Designed by Millions Design
Typeset in 11 on 13pt Garamond by
Cambrian Typesetters, Frimley, Surrey
Origination by Culver Graphics Litho Ltd.
Printed and bound in Belgium by Proost

A CIP catalogue record for this book
is available from the British Library

ISBN 1 85283 164 2

The publishers and author would like to
thank Ralph Titterton and Cathy Ford,
Dan French, Melvin Thomas, Frank Ratcliffe
and Jon Keeble for their invaluable assistance
in the preparation of this book.

Grateful thanks to: Philip Rae for providing the pictures
on pages 50, 53, 60, 61, 62–3, 66, 68, 70, 76 and 77;
Dee Conway/Taylors pages 84, 85 and 87; Gerry Heath
page 93.

CONTENTS

THUNDERBIRDS ARE GO... AGAIN!

People ask me over and over again what made 'Thunderbirds' such an incredible success, not just when it was first shown in the UK some 27 years ago but again during its re-run on BBC2.

I have thought long and hard about this and I have come up with a number of possibilities. The show contains elements that appeal to most children – danger, jeopardy and destruction – but because International Rescue's mission is to save life there is no gratuitous violence. It has a strong family atmosphere where Dad reigns supreme. His sons are always in the forefront of the action and the audience shares his concern for their safety. 'Thunderbirds' is an hour-long show which allows time to introduce new characters, giving the audience the opportunity to get to know and like them before they are put into seemingly hopeless situations. International Rescue then sets about its task and always manages a rescue seconds before time runs out.

However, perhaps the most important reason of all was the dedication of the vast team that worked so tirelessly to make the series. Throughout the filming of 'Thunderbirds' everyone on the production gave it their best shot. No one watched the clock and the studio never seemed to close. It was as though the team sensed they were making something special . . . and of course they were.

So, above all, I believe it was the dedication of all those involved in the production that produced the indefinable magic which has made 'Thunderbirds' a modern classic, and I would like to thank the whole team – wherever they are today – for their truly magnificent contribution. I hope they are as proud of our show as I am.

Finally I would like to express my thanks to editor Penelope Cream, writer John Marriott and researcher Ralph Titterton for the care and attention to detail that has made this book so interesting and informative.

THUNDERBIRDS LIFT OFF

Thunderbirds is a great enigma. Once again the series has astounded with its ability to attract and hold, excite and thrill, as well as intrigue and captivate television audiences of all ages. Small children, teenagers and more mature viewers who affectionately remember the programmes first time around switched on in their millions to watch the series on BBC2. They have been hooked again by the fantastic Thunderbirds space craft, International Rescue, and the perilous missions in which they are engaged.

Since the early days enthusiasm for Thunderbirds has continued to build until it has become one of the most recognised and most talked-about series ever shown on television. The interest is truly international: from the series' earliest days to the present time the ITC Entertainment Group has been successfully licensing the series to television networks throughout the world. Thunderbirds has impressively demonstrated its ageless appeal.

A new generation has now proved its enthusiasm with the high viewing figures and by its clamour for Thunderbirds merchandise.

Exactly what it is that attracts – the exciting storylines, the magic of the puppets, the incredible craft or the extension of unbelievable fantasy into a series of compelling possibility – Thunderbirds continues on its successful path.

It could never have been envisaged that all these years later the series would still be functioning in top gear, enjoying a continuing craze of commitment which right up to the present time truly remains an enigma.

Despite his penchant for innovation and exploiting the latest techniques, Gerry Anderson had not the slightest inkling that 'Thunderbirds' would transfix the public and achieve blast-off in a way that his previous vehicles had not.

Confessing to his limitations as both writer and speller, he and his wife Sylvia went to Portugal to write the pilot script, 'Trapped in the Sky'. Gerry would dictate his ideas, carrying the convolutions of the script in his head. Derek Meddings took his lead for the craft from Gerry's descriptions in this first script, which he dictated to Sylvia over four sessions.

Alan, Brains, Gordon, Scott and Virgil on Tracy Island (left). Scott, seated at Jeff's desk, has taken command in the episode 'Atlantic Inferno', ready to coordinate the craft of International Rescue.

Jeff Tracy, co-ordinator of International Rescue, seated at his desk.

An aerial view of Tracy Island (below).

The weird rescue vehicles, invented by the week for that particular show, as well as Thunderbirds 1–5 themselves, were a fantasy expression of Gerry's fundamental interest in aircraft and spaceships. Whereas it would take the airline industries years to improve on speed, range and the number of passengers carried, Anderson, Meddings and the team could instantly create craft of stunning ability. Intrigued, too, by early space missions, Gerry remembers that when President Kennedy claimed that America would send a man to the moon in ten years Gerry himself prayed that he would live long enough to bear witness to the event.

The secret organisation International Rescue was created by the bottomless pockets of millionaire entrepreneur and ex-astronaut Jeff Tracy; it comprised all manner of state-of-the-art craft and hi-tech gadgetry which would prise individuals from the sort of sticky jams that would have overwhelmed conventional equipment. Working under a thick veil of secrecy on Tracy Island, itself situated non-specifically in the Pacific Ocean, Jeff was spurred on by the sudden death of his wife, which left him with five sons – Scott, Virgil, Alan, Gordon and John – who formed the backbone of his ever-eager rescue squad.

Intelligent and imaginative back-up is provided by the likes of friends-turned-agents (Lady Penelope Creighton-Ward and Jeremiah Turtle *et al.*) who assist the Tracy clan with an effective blend of cunning, caring and charm, while scientific guru and major boffin Hiram K. Hackenbacker (alias Brains) seems only to have to blink through his thick-lensed glasses in order to produce the most advanced scientific wizardry, not to mention the supercharged craft themselves, from thin air. His much-coveted Thunderbirds speed from Tracy Island to the requisite disaster zone, vanish back into the ether and, despite the efforts of an assortment of nasties and ne'er-do-wells, can never be traced right back to base.

The Hood, the key villain throughout the series, is desperate to glean even the slightest detail of the International Rescue operation. The

A portrait of Hiram K. Hackenbacker, more commonly known as 'Brains'.

heartless half-brother of Kyrano, Jeff Tracy's faithful manservant, he is able to influence Kyrano through his disconcerting voodoo-styled hypnotic powers.

However, even the perpetual conniving of the Hood can never penetrate the fortress of Tracy Island. Appearing to the casual eye as merely the paradise home of the Tracy family, its rocks conceal the four Thunderbirds supercraft, while Thunderbird 5 is in a state of constant orbit, picking up Mayday calls from every corner of the globe.

The series took its title, of course, from the five rescue vehicles themselves.

Thunderbird 1 is the supercharged rocket-plane which catapults mission-leader Scott Tracy

towards any danger zone at a speed of 15,000 miles per hour, so that he can make on-site decisions as soon as possible.

Thunderbird 2 is the giant bug-shaped cargo-transporter which carries the appropriate rescue gear in any one of its six huge pods. Virgil Tracy is in command here.

Thunderbird 2 (left) sitting over Pod 5; this large craft can select from a number of pods to help with its rescue missions.

Thunderbird 1 returns to the ship Ocean Pioneer II in the episode 'Danger Ocean Deep' (below).

Thunderbird 3 is a vast spaceship which can effect in-space rescue missions and act as a shuttle to Thunderbird 5. This is in the safe hands of Jeff's youngest son, astronaut Alan Tracy.

Thunderbird 4 is compact enough to be carried in one of the massive pods by Thunderbird 2. A mini-submarine, it hogs centre-stage during underwater emergencies and deep-sea disasters. Gordon Tracy is its aquanaut pilot.

In geo-stationary orbit above the earth, Thunderbird 5 is both space station and communications satellite which is primed to home in on every radio and video signal in the world. Oldest son Scott Tracy is the pilot who can feed instant emergency signals back to his brother Jeff, ready to deal with any crisis.

Thunderbird 5 (above), space station and satellite communications centre, acts as the gathering unit for the world's distress signals.

A real image of the earth is used as the backdrop to this scene of Thunderbird 3 orbiting the planet (left).

Thunderbird 4 tows an underwater well-capping device to stem the flow of oil from the seabed in 'Atlantic Inferno' (right).

EVERY CHARACTER A STACCATO SUPERBRAIN

Though the Thunderbirds themselves upstaged their pilots when either in full flight or mounting a tricky rescue operation, it was the puppets themselves who softened proceedings with their human traits and benevolent tones. Although little background information on each character was squeezed into the series, enough is available to build up a composite picture of each individual.

Jeff Tracy

The lantern jaw and determined frown of Jeff Tracy embody the rugged spirit of the man who founded International Rescue. A thrusting pioneer who would be no stranger to John Wayne, his basic decency caused him to found his squad so as to weed out the assorted rogues and counter the catastrophes regularly bringing the world to the brink of disaster.

As befits his spirit of soaring adventure, Jeff was born and raised on a Kansas wheat farm by a father who combined his sharp mathematical insights with driving a combine harvester for a living. This may well explain Jeff's abiding fascination with complicated machinery as well as his own mathematical prowess.

He carried out his military service with the American air force and progressed smoothly to the rank of colonel before joining the much-fêted Space Agency Project. Here he excelled as an astronaut and his skill and enthusiasm soon enabled him to become one of the first men on the moon.

Jeff's easy ride to fame, glory and space conquest was abruptly ended by the tragic early death of his wife while she was giving birth to their youngest son, Alan. 'Thunderbirds' must have instinctively predicted an era of domesticated New Age men and househusbands when Jeff abandoned his neon-lit space career to return home and bring up his five healthy sons.

A publicity shot of Jeff Tracy, wearing, unusually, Brains' International Rescue uniform.

A Christmas family portrait.

With his mechanical bent well to the fore, Jeff embraced the worlds of civil and construction engineering and, as befits his awesome track record, soon became one of the richest men in the world. Performing an enviable juggling act between work and rearing his children at the same time, his new work also gave him plentiful contacts which would prove useful in the founding of International Rescue, conveniently funded by Jeff's millions.

Jeff Tracy enjoying a game of billiards.

His workaholic nature, entrepreneurial spirit and grand ambition have never diminished his genuine feeling for his fellow-man. Born on 2 January 1970, he's now fifty-six, head of a crack space-age team and showing no signs of slowing down. He has almost to be forced to go to Australia by his offspring when he is offered a much needed break on Lady Penelope's ranch.

Though intelligent, warmhearted and occasionally humorous, Jeff has no trouble at all in being decisive or fixing an errant son with a gimlet eye. In *Thunderbirds Are Go* he rages at Alan for leaving the base unmanned; yet, in a spirit of contradiction which sometimes reveals itself in Jeff, he is applauding the same son by the end of the adventure.

His abiding zeal to improve International Rescue to even the smallest detail gives evidence of an obsessive personality, and Jeff is indeed sometimes irked by his all-out drive. In *Thunderbird 6*, for example, he is frustrated by the conflict between his desire for a further machine and his inability to fathom what its function ought to be. He can, however, be readily boosted by visiting admirers like Tony and Bob Williams in 'Cry Wolf' or Chip in 'Security Hazard'. Whenever a mission is under way, Jeff is firmly in charge on Tracy Island, offering mature middle-aged wisdom to his orbiting sons. Decent to the last, he knows when his hard-working boys are in need of a break and so lets them cut loose for a while. See *Thunderbirds Are Go* for further details. The voice of Jeff Tracy was given full expression by Peter Dyneley.

Scott Tracy

An unsurprising fusion of Dad's intellectual dazzle and gritty masculinity (he reads books and eats steaks), Scott Tracy, born on 14 April 1996, at thirty is the eldest of Jeff's boys. He is admiringly named after the astronaut Scott Malcolm Carpenter. This dark-haired *Wunderkind* was educated at both Yale and Oxford and, like his father before him, joined the United States Air Force where he was decorated on numerous occasions for valour and bravery.

The pilot of Thunderbird 1, the rocket-powered reconnaissance plane whose speed of

15,000 miles per hour matches Scott's lightning brain, he is always first to land at the disaster zone, where he ably assesses the situation and decides what kind of rescue equipment is needed. When it finally arrives, Scott's lack of arrogance enables him to assist in even the most menial tasks. He is also happy to co-pilot Thunderbird 3, where he is of much help to his brother Alan, while his seniority places him firmly in command of the island headquarters whenever his father is absent.

A fast-talking, quick-thinking bright spark who, like his father, enjoys a good joke, he is characterised by a curt decisive speech-pattern, while his final words often trail off into the ether.

As physically powerful as he is knowledgeable, and with the confidence to make instant decisions, he radiates his father's tireless energy and survives on very little sleep. His untroubled nature never dents his determination to win through, while his turquoise uniform and pale sash and band (his on-duty attire) make him instantly recognisable.

His voice was played by actor Shane Rimmer.

Scott Tracy in command on Tracy Island while Jeff is on holiday in Australia, relaxing on Lady Penelope's ranch.

Virgil Tracy

Possessed of an intensity which has by-passed his brothers, Virgil certainly has the most serious nature of all. Born on 15 August 1999, his gravity of demeanour lends him a maturity which obscures his mere twenty-seven years.

An accomplished graduate from the Denver School of Advanced Technology, his mechanical dexterity makes him the ideal pilot of Thunderbird 2, International Rescue's heavy rescue craft and vast transporter. In this capacity, he ends up driving any number of complex vehicles which Thunderbird 2 has brought along for the complicated rescue mission. Just like his brothers, he is never blinded by technology to real human need, and is quite happy to endanger his own life if it means saving others. Virgil takes part in almost every daring encounter in which International Rescue is involved.

Named in tribute to astronaut Virgil Grissom, his looks and colour call his mother to mind, and he thus enjoys an especially close relationship to his father Jeff. Yet Jeff is careful never to let his affection for the young man slide over into favouritism, for that would disrupt the balance and well-being of the entire team.

With medium-brown hair, and sporting a yellow sash and a belt while on duty, he tends towards the monosyllabic. Direct to the point of bluntness, he offers an array of immediate and fixed opinions which are unfailingly correct. Generally fearless and blessed with iron resolve, Virgil does, however, assess the importance of fear without which, he feels, there would be foolhardiness. He believes he owes it to those he is rescuing not to jeopardise their lives in any cavalier act of disregard.

An intriguingly complex creation, Virgil is both music buff gifted pianist and talented artist, and these traditionally non-macho leanings (a debt, perhaps, to his mother) make him a regular butt of his brothers' predictable jokes. Well disposed to the last, Virgil does not, however,

Virgil at the controls of Thunderbird 2, the heavy-duty carrier craft.

hold his brothers in lesser regard. Displaying a particular penchant for jazz, he has also cleverly composed the 'Thunderbirds' rousing theme tune. Barry Gray might thus be a touch confused.

First David Holliday, then, for the second series, Jeremy Wilkin lent their vocal talents to Virgil.

John Tracy

Taking his name from John Glenn, the first American to orbit the earth, John, aged twenty-five, was born on 28 October 2001. With the fair hair and dashing looks of a popular matinée idol, John is certainly the dreamer of the group. This is just as well, since he leads a solitary life aboard Thunderbird 5, International Rescue's space station which is in a state of permanent orbit, high above Earth. It has to be properly manned so that distress signals, picked up by Thunderbird 5 from frequencies across the globe, can be beamed back to base and so kick-start the team into their rescue missions.

His time at Harvard University gave him a superb knowledge of electronics and specialist skills in laser communications, while he also trained as an astronaut. The quietest and most intellectual of all the boys, he also shares his father's active interest in astronomy. His sealed-off existence in Thunderbird 5 allows him ample opportunity to pursue his hobby, while his natural patience is a prerequisite of the job.

The discovery of the quasar system is accredited to John, as are four substantial textbooks on astronomy and outer space. A slightly dour character, his intellectual abilities outshine his action-man experience, and he rarely participates in an actual rescue mission, a worthy exception being 'Danger at Ocean Deep'. John is, however, athletically able and, despite his slightly less muscular build, received many athletics awards at school which he naturally attributes to sheer mental agility. His brother Alan replaces John on Thunderbird 5 for a month at a time, when he assumes command of Alan's Thunderbird 3.

Wearing a lilac sash and belt, John's voice is given life by long-term Anderson associate Ray Barrett.

John Tracy answers an emergency call at the controls of Thunderbird 5.

Gordon Tracy in the cockpit of Thunderbird 4, the small versatile submarine craft of the International Rescue fleet.

Gordon Tracy

Born on 14 February 2004, Gordon is distinguished by both frivolous banter and a sense of perky fun which place him attractively at odds with the harsh intensity of Virgil and the intellectual dreaming of John. Whether teasing his younger brother Alan about being in love, as in 'End of the Road', or embarking on some other joky escapade, he is often rebuked by his stern father.

Yet he is a keen contributor to the rescue team who can switch from light-hearted antics to committed responsibility in a flash. He is, in fact, the skilled aquanaut in charge of Thunderbird 4, a highly versatile submarine which is suitably equipped with top-strength underwater lighting, powerful cutting gear and a flexible grappling-hook. Thunderbird 4 is usually transported to the rescue site by Thunderbird 2.

This auburn-haired blue-eyed twenty-two-year-old undersea specialist has a particular affinity with water and has an unsurprising liking for all kinds of water-sports from water-skiing to skin-diving.

Named after astronaut Leroy Gordon Cooper, he became an expert on oceanography in the Submarine Service and World Aquanaut Security Patrol where he invented a breakthrough underwater breathing apparatus, an improved version of which is employed in the exclusive service of International Rescue. With a strength and tenacity which underlie his good-natured high spirits, Gordon is one of the world's fastest freestyle swimmers and, in fact, won an Olympic medal for the butterfly stroke. At WASP, Gordon was put in command of a bathyscaphe in which he spent a year underwater so as to study seabed life and marine farming methods. A short time before International Rescue began to function, he survived a dreadful crash in his hydrofoil speedboat which capsized at 400 knots and was completely destroyed on impact. After spending four months in a hospital bed, Gordon returned to action with high spirits reined in a bit and a healthy new respect for the sea, though he will always remain the team's greatest prankster. He can be picked out by an orange sash and belt and the voice of David Graham.

Alan Tracy

A blond-haired baby-face who is as reckless as he is romantic, twenty-one-year-old Alan is the youngest of the brothers. Born on 12 March 2005, he was named after Alan B. Shephard, the first man to play golf on the moon, which Alan himself has visited many times. Aside from carrying out his stints aboard Thunderbird 5, he is the astronaut mainly responsible for Thunderbird 3 and is assisted in this task by Scott. He studied at Harvard University where he developed a rocket and, much to the annoyance of his tutors, actually launched it. It veered right off course, shattering every window at the University of Colorado. Jeff then decided that, in order to teach his impulsive son a sense of responsibility, Alan should also train as an astronaut, and his subsequent success in that field has borne out Jeff's faith in him.

Though a terrific sportsman, partygoer and racing-car driver (this latter enthusiasm lands him in trouble in 'Move and You're Dead'), he enjoys the quiet contemplations of archaeology and regularly wanders off to the less visible corners of Tracy Island to pore over rocks and potholes. This never interferes, however, with his utter dedication to International Rescue and to his father, who nevertheless sometimes treats him like a wayward schoolboy.

Such friction is highly visible in 'The Perils of Penelope' and *Thunderbirds Are Go*.

Though it is never fully written into any one script, Alan, the misty dewy-eyed romantic of the family, does seem to be involved with Tin-Tin, the daughter of the Tracys' loyal man-servant Kyrano. He is, in fact, the only brother in love with another of the characters. We only see evidence of this supposed relationship through Tin-Tin's attention to other men. In 'End of the Road', an old family friend, Eddie Houseman, visits the base and causes Tin-Tin to gasp in admiration. Alan's short-fuse jealousy is calmed by Grandma, whose mix of tact and gentle conniving brings the twosome back together again. Though also having to woo Tin-Tin back in 'The Cham Cham', where she gushes over Cass Carnaby, or in 'Ricochet', where she is transfixed by a mere mortal, Alan has learned neither to take her for granted nor to confuse her

Alan Tracy, youngest of the brothers, is pilot of Thunderbird 3 and rotates monitor duty aboard Thunderbird 5 with John.

A rare portrait of Lady Penelope Creighton-Ward.

FAB 1, Lady Penelope's pink Rolls-Royce, leaving Glen Fields airbase.

with the furniture. Despite his sex appeal as an impulsive blond bombshell, he remains single, the clue to which may be his giveaway remark in *Thunderbird 6*: 'The life I lead at International Rescue is too dangerous to ask anyone to share it with me.'

Voiced by Matt Zimmerman, he sports a fetching off-white sash and belt which are a perfect match for his stunning blond hairdo.

Lady Penelope

Born on 24 December 1999, and voiced by Sylvia Anderson, Lady Penelope Creighton-Ward is a twenty-seven-year-old aristocrat who is the key member of International Rescue's all-important network of undercover agents. Working from her large stately home in rural Kent, she is the globe-trotting British agent for International Rescue whose top-drawer elegance stands in amusing contrast to her constant girlish craving for intrigue. Her travels for International Rescue include tracking down a pack of criminals in 'The Imposters', opening a road in 'Atlantic Inferno' and dazzling all at a party to celebrate the success of a solar generator.

A grand lady who even had her own comic strip in *TV21*, she appears to those ignorant of her secret life as someone who really lives for lunch, yet she is a tough, if always charming, adversary to those who would disrupt world peace.

Polite and well mannered to the last, she is both a chic dresser who follows world fashion and a big-hearted altruist who will always bring help of all kinds to beleaguered unfortunates. Like her willing crook-turned-sidekick Parker, she has a child's enthusiam for electronic gadgets and, even if they can only perform the simplest task, will at once install them in her house or pink Rolls-Royce, FAB 1, which transports the odd couple on relaxing excursions in the countryside.

The only other luxury transport in her life is FAB 2, a yacht she enjoys on global jaunts. It was one of those trips which enabled her to meet Jeff Tracy, who, seeking an agent in Europe, was enchanted by Lady Penelope, who was already active as a successful spy. Jeff insisted she tackle a very difficult test and, after she succeeded with great ease and aplomb, he invited her on board. Her cool poise and steel nerves help her in the behind-the-scenes handywork which has pushed many an International Rescue mission towards triumph.

Aside from a distaste for American coffee, this single-minded pursuer of all hardened criminals is frightened witless by mice (see 'The Mighty Atom' for evidence of this). This fear combines amusingly with her upper-crust preference for

Lady Penelope in the drawing room of her stately mansion, which was based on Stourhead House in Mere, Wiltshire.

understatement to create fun moments in the midst of adventure: in *Thunderbirds Are Go* she explains to Parker, 'I don't think there is much need in looking for survivors,' or 'Oh dear, just when I am expecting visitors – three coach-loads, too. How inconvenient.' Her persistence and top-drawer Englishness are effectively satirised in 'Day of Disaster', where she declares firmly 'In my house everything stops for tea.'

Zena Relph, couturier to Lady Penelope, recalls the puppet and the period with great affection.

'I first became involved with Gerry when I replaced the wardrobe mistress on "Fireball XL5" when she went down with measles. I was, in fact, a floor puppeteer on "Stingray", before being asked to dress Lady Penelope for "Thunderbirds". Along with Sylvia and Betty Coleman, I'd leaf through *Vogue* for suitably exotic outfits, which appeared on Lady Penelope at the rate of one a week. The costumes were always made of silk, wool or cotton so that they would move with the body.'

A full-time magician, who once worked on a Russian cruise ship, Zena recently designed an off-white wool dress and re-created the mink coat from *Thunderbirds Are Go* for Lady Penelope's starring role in a Swinton Insurance commercial.

Parker

Born on 30 May, and possibly fifty-two years of age, Parker is Lady Penelope's sidekick who has been transformed from seedy crook into loyal butler, chauffeur and all-in-one aid. The joint appearance of Parker and Penelope in the pages of *TV21* gives us background knowledge of their relationship. It seems they met when Parker was trying to steal Penelope's car but was foiled by an anti-theft alarm. Instead of being handed over at once to the police, Parker, much to his surprise, was recruited by Lady Penelope, who could readily spot a resourceful ex-con, even if initially she had to press Parker into service with the help of a gun. The television series does, however, suggest that they may have joined forces after Penelope's assiduous trawling of the underworld for a useful assistant. For Penelope to be of value to the Tracy boys, and be able to squash criminals underfoot, she sometimes has to slide gracefully to just the wrong side of the law where Parker can help her pick locks and blow safes.

Blessed with the slightly surreal first name of Aloysius, but better known to his former associates as Nosey on account of his most obvious facial trait, Parker is reputed to be the best safe-blower in the world and has a reputation for unswerving loyalty and sound mechanical ability, which proves useful in tinkering with FAB 1.

Penelope's seductive charm and gentle persuasion eventually sent Parker down the road of total devotion to ' 'er Ladyship', and he was never once offended by her insistence on educating him in matters of etiquette. In the manner of a broad cockney, he is apt to preface all vowels with 'h', as in 'hinformation' and 'hadmiration'. Yet Parker's origins still betray themselves when it comes to food (in 'Vault of Death' he pronounces to Lilly the cook: 'Stew – me favourite'), and he can never quite shake off his grubby associates. They can either provide much

A rare picture (above) of Parker at Scott's mobile control – perhaps waiting for his cue during the production of a 'Thunderbirds' episode...

useful information or alternatively cause trouble, as does Light-Fingered Fred in 'Vault of Death', in which Parker is torn between loyalty to his new cause and to his former associates. In fact it is the conflict between his new social position and his rough past, as evidenced in his convoluted speech-patterns, which constitutes the best comedy in the series.

Although Parker was initially conceived as simple dramatic support to Lady Penelope, he would actively upstage her on many occasions because of his intrinsic amusement value. He would become more popular with many fans than even the dashing superheroes and was indeed the favourite character of Gerry Anderson himself.

While Gerry & Co. were still at the planning stage of 'Thunderbirds', they would regularly visit a traditional English pub near Cookham called the King's Arms. They were often served by a very decent waiter named Arthur, who had once been in the Queen's service at Windsor Castle and, in the appreciative manner of Parker enjoying his new liaison with upper-crust England, would give detailed accounts of life with Her Majesty. A wonderfully rich, lively character, Arthur was assiduously studied by David Graham who, once he had been selected as the voice of Parker, visited the pub on a number of occasions. With identical vocal and

A portrait of reformed ex-con Aloysius 'Nosey' Parker, now butler to Lady Penelope.

other mannerisms to Parker, Arthur never knew he had become an international hero; and Gerry, sensing that Arthur would not be best pleased at such vast recognition, never summoned up the courage to tell him. Gerry even believes that such knowledge would have destroyed Arthur who, unwitting to the end, sadly died a few years later.

Actor and voice artist David Graham, who is an accomplished veteran of the theatres of London's West End, the National Theatre and the BBC, first met Gerry when he was playing a villain in a television film, directed by Gerry, for the Martin Caine series. 'I was just a working character actor. I'd always been good at voices and, when Jerry said he hoped to do a puppet-based production, I said I'd like to give it a try. Before "Thunderbirds", in fact, I did "Four Feather Falls", "Supercar". "Fireball XL5" and "Stingray".'

Although he gave life to Gordon, Brains and Kyrano, David will always be linked with Parker in the public imagination. David admits that he 'never dreamed Parker would become a cult figure, though, along with Brains, he's certainly my favourite character. I created a fantasy life for him and indeed revived him last year when Gerry was making a charity speech at the Grosvenor House Hotel. Gerry had a model set with Parker on it, and my pre-recorded dialogue, which was in pure Parkerese, was pumped into the room.'

Lady Penelope and Parker relax at Bonga Bonga, Penelope's Australian ranch.

Brains

A loving parody of a teenage boy wonder, Brains is the glum bespectacled inventor of all the dazzling machines for International Rescue and is, when he has a spare moment, currently translating Einstein's theory of relativity into Latin.

Though not one of the Tracy family, he none the less brings complementary brainpower to their collective skills, and, self-critical to the last, he is never at ease with his creations and is consequently often to be found modifying and tinkering with his machines. Never to be found scuba-diving or chasing Tin-Tin, his off-duty relaxation includes the study of trigonometry and thermodynamics, while he is forever cooking up new and radical ideas for improving Brainman, a robot who once beat him at chess.

Reduced to the status of orphan when a hurricane destroyed his Michigan home, Brains was twelve years old when he was adopted by a professor at the University of Cambridge who immediately found evidence of Brains's analytical prowess and dazzling intellect. Nothing proved too overwhelming for Brains to absorb or learn.

Jeff Tracy, after he had conceived International Rescue, realised that a switched-on superbrain would be necessary to help him accomplish his plans, and went on an extended world tour in search of a genius. Jeff eventually descended on Paris, where Brains was nervously delivering a deep-delving high-octane lecture in a palace of culture and knew at once that this was the man for him. Brains, acknowledging that Jeff was a decent entrepreneur who could save mankind, accepted Jeff's mighty challenge without pause for thought.

Neither Brains's intense bespectacled stare nor his nervous stutter prevent him reacting to the pressure of circumstance, so that he is able both to advise the others ('Pit of Peril', 'Day of Disaster', 'Sun Probe', *Thunderbirds Are Go*) and find the courage to join in ('Lord Parker's Oliday', *Thunderbird 6*). In the midst of gung-ho astronauts and whizzing supercraft, Brains is a comforting island of comic solemnity.

The voice of Brains was provided by David Graham.

Brains, genius behind Jeff's dream of International Rescue.

Kyrano

Like Brains and Parker before him, Kyrano is voiced by David Graham and displays the same touching loyalty to Jeff and the boys, to whom he has been manservant for such a long time that he has also become Jeff's friend. Of Malaysian extraction, he feels that there is nothing he would not do for his masters and exudes a relaxing warmth to all around him. Like most others in the cast, Kyrano is one of the world's finest in his chosen skill, which in his case happens to be botany. Kyrano did, in fact, spend several years at Kew Gardens, where, as a consultant botanist, he advised on Asian orchids.

Kyrano was once active at the Kennedy Space Center where Jeff first met him. Already predisposed towards the adventurous world of astronauts, he was engaged in the discovery of ways of producing synthetic food from plants which could then be concentrated into tablet or paste forms to feed astronauts. This experience was a launch-pad for Kyrano, who quickly became a culinary wizard, and such was his excellence that he was soon installed as head chef at the Paris Hilton. Needless to say, Jeff and the boys eat well at all times.

Kyrano's father made sizeable fortunes from his vast estates and rubber plantations, but Kyrano himself, instead of inheriting his right and proper share of his father's will, was tricked out of his wealth by his malevolent half-brother, the Hood. It is the Hood who exposes Kyrano's minor flaw by exerting a sometimes mesmeric hold over him, and he is quite happy to exploit Kyrano's good nature by using him as an unwitting pawn in his prolonged attempts to crush International Rescue. Kyrano, however, has long since reacted against his half-brother's greed by replacing any interest in the material world with an enthusiasm for inner harmony, and this he has certainly found on Tracy Island.

The Hood

The Hood, so named after his inventive array of disguises, was thus able to offer endless dramatic possibilities to the script-writing team. Abusing his hypnotic inexplicable power over his kindly half-brother, Kyrano, he can often temporarily outwit the Tracy brothers, whom he will try to thwart as often as possible so as to glean the priceless plans of Thunderbirds 1–5.

Never referred to as 'the Hood' as such in the series, he creates harrowing disasters which are designed to trap the Tracys; yet, even with the element of surprise on his side, he can only ever come close to securing the prized plans. In 'Martian Invasion', for example, after filming Thunderbirds 1 and 2, he speeds off to a potential buyer but is forcibly stopped in his tracks by the Tracys.

He is feared as the world's foremost villain and, in complete contrast to the gentle features of Kyrano, he has a hard evil stare which is accentuated by outsize eyebrows and a mean, chiselled face. A huge man who can reduce the innocent to jelly by simply standing still, he is chiefly interested in dispensing with truth, justice and all things civilised in his mad pursuit of vast wealth. If only he had his huge hands on those Thunderbirds blueprints, he would auction them to the highest bidder.

The Hood, though generally working alone from his hard-to-locate temple in the bowels of the Malaysian jungle, is quite prepared to use unsavoury riff-raff and maladjusted lawbreakers to achieve his aim, and he can be seen causing much trouble in, for example, 'Trapped in the

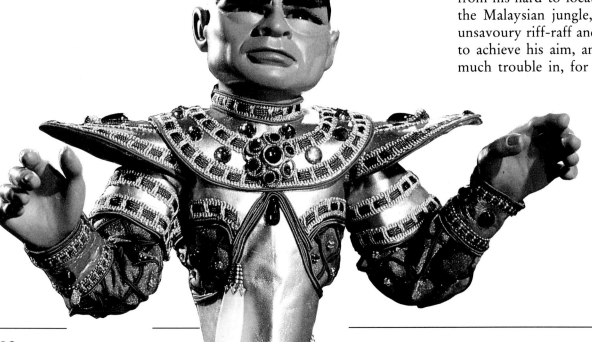

Tin-Tin (right), Kyrano's daughter, and the Hood (left), Kyrano's half-brother, work on opposite sides; Tin-Tin is loyal to International Rescue while the Hood plots to obtain its secrets.

Sky', 'Martian Invasion', 'The Edge of Impact' and 'Desperate Intruder'. As ruthless and unfeeling as he is expert in voodoo and black magic, he will willingly trample on all those around him should the need arise, and he is often engaged in blackmail to keep his whereabouts secret. Though he is blown up for good in *Thunderbirds Are Go*, his enduring strength and naked ambition enable him to descend magically from the ether in time for his appearance as the Black Phantom in *Thunderbird 6*.

Tin-Tin

Tin-Tin, whose name is Malaysian for 'sweet', is the enigmatic daughter of Kyrano and therefore unlikely half-niece of the Hood. Embodying, like all the others, the pervasive heavy emphasis on solid family values and a decent education, she was educated in America and Europe at the insistence of Jeff, who incurred the expense because of her father's loyal devotion.

After graduation, she joined International Rescue and became unwittingly involved in the very first rescue mission, 'Trapped in the Sky',

where a nuclear bomb is discovered on board the Fireflash aircraft on which she is travelling. She is also involved in 'Sun Probe; and 'The Cham Cham' in which she helps Lady Penelope.

Her high-level knowledge of mathematics, engineering and complex technical theories makes her an ideal choice as assistant to Brains, and the genius twosome can often be seen grappling with an advance laboratory experiment. Strictly supervising the maintenance of all the organisation's machines, she has thus repaid Jeff's kindness in funding her education. As fashion-conscious as Lady Penelope (Tin-Tin designs her own clothes) and as robustly athletic as Gordon (she particularly enjoys water-skiing and swimming), Tin-Tin combines the passive femininity of the East with the free-thinking determination of the West. Susceptible, too, to romance, she is dazzled by Alan, who is glued to her side, yet she tweaks his nerve-ends by jolting him out of his complacency and on to his toes. Alan is consequently both intoxicated by and disturbed in love.

Grandma

Perhaps old age has got to Grandma since, although she is taken to Tracy Island by Alan Tracy in 'Move and You're Dead', where she is introduced to viewers, she had actually graced 'Sun Probe', a much earlier episode, with her presence.

Forgetful or not, she weaves her way in and out of the series and is primarily a dramatic cipher who feeds lines to the principals in order to move proceedings on. Never actually confirmed on screen as Jeff Tracy's mother, she is, however, presumed to be such, is drawn in sketchily and is sometimes taken for granted by her fellow-puppets. Yet she does mastermind a clever solution to secure the release of a helpless bank clerk who is trapped in a Bank of England vault. With the knowledge that an abandoned underground railway line passes conveniently beneath the vault, Grandma suggests to the boys that they blast their way in from the railway line to the bank. She is not really given credit for her well-hatched plan and so is the only character in the series not to be continually applauded for her resourcefulness and intelligence.

HOW TO SAVE THE WORLD

Jeff Tracy had originally planned his operations so that Thunderbirds 1–5 would undertake all the heavy work. While Thunderbirds 1 and 2 could cope with both the air and the ground, Thunderbird 3 specialised in space, Thunderbird 4 in water, while Thunderbird 5 was an orbiting satellite which picked up distress signals from across the globe and fed them back to base. There must, however, also have been a mystery satellite to home in on that side of the planet which Thunderbird 5 was incapable of covering.

Jeff soon learned that, because of the complex variations in rescue operations, more equipment would be necessary, and one brand-new rescue vehicle a week became a thrilling highlight of each show, transported to the danger zone by Thunderbird 2 in its hangar-shaped pods.

Thunderbird 1 is perhaps the most striking and invigorating of all the craft. With blue base, dynamic rocket body and purposeful red nose, it is always first to launch from Tracy Island, and its superior speed enables it to reach the rescue zone first. Then decisions can be made by Scott as to how the rescue can be best effected. In case of unsavoury threats, Thunderbird 1 is also fully armed.

In order to simplify Scott's tasks at high speed, all of Thunderbird 1's controls are automatic where possible. The check-lights which grace the top of the panel are set above a multi-purpose television screen on which normal communication, route maps and touchdown conditions can be readily projected. Thrust and flight controls are mounted conveniently on both arms of Scott's swing-seat, which will change position automatically to keep him upright during the dramatic switch from vertical to horizontal flight.

Also armed is Thunderbird 2, which, decked out in suitably utilitarian green, is not only the principal heavy-duty craft but also the transporter of a complex array of rescue gear. With its red engines blasting at full tilt, it speeds through the ether.

Scott Tracy shifts Thunderbird 1 into horizontal flight on its way to another rescue site.

Thunderbird 1 roars into the sky from its secret hangar beneath the swimming pool.

Designed for space rescue and as a shuttle to the far-flung Thunderbird 5, Thunderbird 3 is a thrusting orange rocket whose three distinctive fins support the three rocket engines at the base.

Thunderbird 4's gleaming yellow fuselage allows it to stand out under water, where it undertakes all of International Rescue's watery rescue work. The smallest of all the rescue craft, it also has a mobile lighting trough at the front which can probe the murkiest corners of the seabed, as well as a batch of high-tech extendable equipment and weapons which can be used when the trough is lowered.

Thunderbird 5 is International Rescue's circular space station which, aside from banks of necessary receiving equipment, also has a docking hatch and docking ramp for Thunderbird 3. Its silver body is encircled by a copper ring.

Since solitary periods in space can place John under great strain, luxury rest facilities have been thoughtfully provided in Thunderbird 5. Attractive features include a huge television screen and a well-stocked film library; soothing circular shapes embrace the contours of the craft, the central table, the comfy sofa and easy chair, the last thoughtfully provided with foot-rest. Any number of drinks can silently emerge from beneath the table at the mere touch of a button.

John's concealed record-player, shelves of books and single pot-plant, which is growing in nutrient solution (horticulture being a favourite hobby of John's) all add to the super-soothing ambience. All-round air-conditioning ensures that John does not break into a sweat during his policing of the world's distress calls.

A high-grade computer assists him in this task. Programmed to select all messages which contain words like 'help', 'emergency' and 'rescue' in every conceivable language, it then transmits them to every corner of the satellite so that John cannot possibly miss any of them. John, needless to say, spends much of his time in orbit in the study of languages.

Although John's days are usually spent alone, at times he rotates his monitoring duties with his youngest brother, Alan. During these periods, John takes command of the speedier craft Thunderbird 3, adopting for a month at a time a quite different role in the emergency missions of International Rescue.

John monitors the world's communications aboard the Thunderbird 5 satellite.

A major part of the weekly international thrill was due to the intoxicating launch procedures, even though they employed stock footage which was dropped in time and again. Grasping that only tiny models were going through a complex sequence of tricky motions, emulating the speed and vapour of real craft only added to the enthralment of a global audience.

Passed through a sequence like a chocolate bar in a space-age wrapping factory, Scott stands on the revolving floor and wall in the Tracy lounge. His hands clutch the two wall-lamps, which in turn activate the wall and spin him right round into the bay of Thunderbird 1. The wall assumes its normal position, Scott stands on a gantry platform which instantly feeds him out towards the rocket. The gantry touches the nose, the door panel slides open and the pilot steps on to the chair footplate. He sits in the chair, which revolves to face the other way. With well-oiled slickness, the door closes, the gantry retracts and

Thunderbird 1 moves effortlessly down a chute on a bogie, inching its way beneath the house itself. Now ensconced in its blast-proof launch-bay, Thunderbird 1 gets ready to blast its way through the swimming-pool which adorns the front of the Tracy villa.

The pool works hydraulically and conveniently moves silently to one side to get out of Scott's way so that he can promptly vanish towards the danger zone. Once airborne, he announces his successful lift-off to his father via his own portrait, which along with those of his brothers, is mounted on a wall opposite his father's desk. When at work, the boys appear in these photos in uniform and sash; when not, the cover-up photos turn the boys into a semblance of relaxed professional golfers. With Scott having switched to horizontal flight, he can readily manipulate the movable wings (a feature guaranteed to generate alarm on most conventional aircraft) which can both increase stability and enable

vertical landings and lift-offs. In 'Trapped in the Sky', for example, Scott announces to the British commander at London Airport that he has no need of a runway but can land vertically instead.

For Virgil, the build-up to the launch of Thunderbird 2 is much more dramatic. As he stands to attention in front of a picture of a rocket in the Tracy lounge, the picture tilts him back so that his feet are higher than his head and slides him on a custom-built padded trolley right into the cockpit of Thunderbird 2. With the picture now back in place, Virgil reaches a point in the journey where the chute levels out and he is spun round on a mini-turntable so that he is now feet-first. The turntable tilts up, and Virgil is propelled down the chute into his pilot seat which, when his feet strike a footplate, springs up and frees the chute. The seat clicks on to a seat column, and the chute vanishes out of the door.

Virgil now sets in motion the conveyor belt which carries the six huge green pods underneath the craft. Each pod contains various rescue apparatus. Once he has selected the required

This publicity shot shows Thunderbird 1 with its wings open; this normally only takes place when the craft is in horizontal flight and nearing its destination.

pod, Virgil lets his craft squat down on it and he clamps it into place. While this has been going on, the cliff-face which hides Thunderbird 2 slides down, while two rows of palm trees obediently bend over to give Thunderbird 2 the required wing-clearance. Had the trees never been planted, the wide airstrip would have given an obvious clue to the whereabouts of International Rescue. The trees, which are planted in a nutrient solution, are located alongside fire-fighting sprays which rise from the ground when Thunderbird 2 needs to be doused down after an emergency landing as in 'Terror in New York City' when a World Navy ship, realising that Thunderbird 2 is too slow to be a missile but too quick for an aeroplane, yet knowing nothing of International Rescue, launches an attack.

Its heavy bulk moves slowly along the airstrip-road, comes to a halt and is then elevated forty-five degrees in the air by hydraulic pumps which push that particular section of road skywards. A smaller road section to the rear of Thunderbird 2 also opens up to take the full blast from the craft and thus conceal any signs of lift-off. Like Scott in Thunderbird 1, Virgil can quickly switch to vertical manoeuvres.

Should International Rescue be required when visitors are present on Tracy Island, Jeff has absolutely no problem in steering them towards soundproofed windowless rooms, where they remain until launch procedures are over, completely unaware and content in the lap of luxury.

The most amusing launch of all occurs when a travelling sofa propels (normally) Scott and Alan towards Thunderbird 3. With the boys ensconced in the sofa in the middle of the living-room, Jeff

The heavy transporter, Thunderbird 2, prepares to follow Thunderbird 1 to the scene of action, carrying one of the various pod-contained vehicles which are piloted by Virgil (below).

touches a button which sends them down to an underground chamber. The settee now adorns a trolley on rails, a duplicate model shoots upwards into Jeff's living-room, where a missing sofa might raise eyebrows. The first trolley stops, the sofa glides on to another ramp which pushes Scott, Alan and sofa inside the rocket. The ramp returns to the base of the rocket, while the boys are taken up into the cockpit by lift. They have never left the sofa at any stage, except to pilot Thunderbird 3 from within its comforts.

Thunderbird 3 takes off through the oddly shaped Round House that sports a concealed hollow centre which, even when revealed, is still only visible from the air.

Thunderbird 4 is normally carried to any danger zone in Pod 4 by Thunderbird 2. Hovering above the water, Thunderbird 2 simply drops Pod 4 into the water, where it floats; a door opens and Thunderbird 4 is launched on rails into the water. On completion of its mission, the yellow one-man submarine climbs back up the rails into the pod where it finally swivels round on a turntable in readiness for its next escapade.

However, if need be, Thunderbird 4 can be launched from Tracy Island on a slipway which is actually Thunderbird 2's launch-ramp. It can also be launched into the sea from a jetty at the end of the road. 'Terror in New York City' bears witness to this latter procedure where, after the World Navy has impeded the operations of International Rescue, Jeff insists on sending Thunderbird 4 to New York. The only moments of drama in which Thunderbird 5 is involved occur when Thunderbird 3 docks at the static spaceship.

The craft themselves are matched by the pink dazzle of FAB 1, Lady Penelope's gadget-heavy Rolls-Royce which is driven at all times by Parker. It must sniff out criminals more effectively than a tracker dog, for in 'Trapped in the Sky', where Jeff informs Penelope that The

Thunderbird 3, largest of the craft, soars into space (left).

Thunderbird 4 launches into the sea from Pod 4. In 'Operation Crash Dive' (left) Thunderbird 4 cuts the engines from the stricken Fire Flash allowing it to float to the surface and the crew to be rescued.

A rare production shot of FAB 1 outside a table-top set of Creighton Manor; clearly visible is the camber which allows the camera to film on ground level while increasing the perspective.

opening night of *Thunderbirds FAB* at London's Mermaid Theatre.

The car which acts as a fitting symbol for Parker's cockney comedy and Lady Penelope's undiluted class was a complex creation. Three sizes of the shocking-pink Rolls were constructed for the series. The large vehicle was complemented by both a tiny six-inch model and a six-foot puppet-size version, the latter being used most of the time. At least as much a star as the glamorous Thunderbird 1 or the comical Thunderbird 2, FAB 1 was constructed by professional model-maker Wag Evans who, now as then, is still employed by Space Models. He acknowledges that the puppet-size model, which preceded the smaller one, was a masterpiece of engineering. So that interior shots could be composed, the car had to come apart at the front and at the rear, as well as at each side. The two sides of the canopy could be lifted off, while the doors could open and slide neatly underneath. The car also had to be able to move, steer and fire off its grille-covered machine-gun in realistic fashion.

With substantial wooden tops for each wing, the car was mainly built from plywood. The wheels, with their wooden disc centres, and the vac-formed tyres were held together with the aid of a black rubber bag. Turned aluminium was employed for the hub-caps. Wag can recall using brass which he then chrome-plated for both the radiator and the miniature Flying Lady mascot, though on completion he was annoyed by the presence of a dull straight line between the wheel arches. Wag spent a great deal of time actually constructing FAB 1 and, bringing the space age down to street-level, he remembers buying its battery-driven headlamps from a bicycle shop. In fact he used only the rim and reflectors.

FAB 1 was only once in need of repair, when the two tubes which held it together at the section joins needed to be replaced. So the puppets could be re-dressed for different scenes, the underside of the car was removable. The larger FAB 1, which was a mobile means of promoting the series, is now kept at the Cars of the Stars Motor Museum in Keswick.

FAB 1, supposedly designed by Brains, who attempted to render it completely indestructible, can also function as a hydrofoil, though Lady P

Hood is speeding through England in her vicinity (she supposedly resides in rural Kent), she is on his tail moments later, heading toward Birmingham on the M1. However, these minor aberrations only ever added to the prevailing spirit of lunacy.

Decked out in unique Penelope fluorescent pink, and with Parker's central driving position and clear roof contributing to its futuristic feel, it contains much to amuse the gadget-happy agent. One of the machine-guns pops out from behind the radiator grille (it zaps and fries The Hood's speeding car in 'Trapped in the Sky'), while missile-launchers, rear-mounted grappling-hooks and oil-slick ejectors are also a great boon.

The design of FAB 1 had to be scrutinised by Rolls-Royce, who offered their keen support. Gerry Anderson recalls that the six-foot Rolls cost about £2,500 (the equivalent of around £30,000 today); while, at £10,000, the full-size working prop cost more then than a real Rolls-Royce. This vehicle made an appearance at the prefers her huge luxury yacht, FAB 2, for her aquatic adventures. It features heavily in 'The Man from MI5' where Penelope and Parker are tracking a pack of criminals, only to become trapped and in need of rescuing themselves. Despite also requiring Jeff's help in 'The Perils of Penelope' and 'The Duchess Assignment', his tolerant support means that he has never once complained. Cool even in the heat of danger, Penelope's chief worry when FAB 1 is under attack is: 'I hope they don't scratch the paint, Parker.'

The Anderson effects and writing team knew how to capture the viewers' enthusiasm and imagination by introducing a battery of specialist rescue vehicles, many of whose thuggish industrial appearances contrast convincingly with the space-age streamlining of Thunderbirds 1–5. A dramatic contrast was provided when the smooth slab-sided Thunderbird 2 released a vehicle from its pod, all broken surfaces and jutting hardware.

These vehicles complemented Thunderbirds 1–5 in that they could support walls, fight fires or bore underground. Perhaps the most inspirational of all the machines is the Mole, which, in the manner of a giant drill, can rescue those hapless civilians who are trapped underground.

The cutaway drawing of FAB 1, first seen in the 1965 Summer Extra edition of *TV21* magazine.

FAB 1 Lady Penelope's ROLLS-ROYCE
as seen in 'THUNDERBIRDS'.

Hydraulic platform with fold down safety rails.

Driving position showing the incredibly un-complicated controls for such a complex vehicle.

Swivel laser beam and smoke making apparatus. Set in rear wings.

Gull wing canopy and down-and-under doors.

Laminated, Anti-glare, bullet-proof glass-steel canopy.

Part of the top secret enormously powerful engine

Retro pack air brakes (fitted to both wings — indicated on off-side wing only.)

Rear Hydrofoil.

The hub cap motif extends on rod to form a tyre slasher. (On all wheels — foremost shown in normal position.)

Retractable studs for snow and ice. (Shown on one wheel only—fitted to all six).

Centre pull down armrests of back seat have retractable handcuffs and chest band.

Hydrofoils when fully lowered extend below level of wheels thus lifting whole car clear of water when at speed—minimizes resistance. The rear 'foil has a vortex-aquajet powerpack fitted centrally.

FOLLOWING many requests to TV 21 asking for details of Lady Penelope's Rolls-Royce, the Editor has finally secured permission to reveal some of the interesting features which have hitherto remained **top secret**.
The design of FAB 1 has been officially approved by the Rolls-Royce Company but its main power unit must remain on the classified data list. Speeds in excess of 200 m.p.h. have been attained but it is certain that this is only a modest estimate of the engine's real potential.
The four front wheels have been incorporated in the design to support the weight of the power unit and also the heavy machine guns which are retractable and ready for use at the push of a button.
The car has no driving mirror but relies on a small television monitor screen on its dashboard which receives a TV image from the camera concealed in the boot.
Normal television transmitters and receivers, plus UHF and Neutroni radio units are installed within the completely air conditioned car for immediate contact to and from the vehicle.
When FAB 1 parks all six wheels rotate until the car is able to drive into its parking space sideways.

© 1965 City Magazines Ltd. & A.P. Films (Merchandising) Ltd.

ITC world wide distribution

The Mole, International Rescue's burrowing machine (left), designed to tunnel through the hardest rock.

Transported to the rescue site by Thunderbird 2 in Pod 4, the Mole travels on its own trolley which, on arrival, tips upwards to near-vertical position; a rocket fires at the rear to activate the Mole, which begins to turn its massive screw and burrow underground. Weighing in at thirty tons and powered by a nuclear reactor, its nose is made from Formula C30/1, a super-strength metal dreamed up by Brains, while the heavy-duty caterpillar tracks enable it to grip the sides of the tunnel it is boring and so return to the surface in safety.

Dramatic participation by the Mole can be seen in 'City of Fire', where a family is trapped by fire in the basement of the world's tallest building, Thompson Tower; while in 'Pit of Peril' it rescues the American army's brand-new Sidewinder from the bowels of a Second World War disposal-pit. Furthermore, it saves the distressed Duchess of Royston from the cellar of an old mansion in 'The Duchess Assignment'.

Derek Meddings generously gives credit for many of these vehicles to a young artist called Michael Trim who, he says, drew excellent storyboards. Busy running three stages with three directors, Derek let Michael, who could be seen drawing at all times of the day, even during his lunch-break, complete many designs. Derek would give him vehicles to design and, although Derek received credit for all of them, there were times when Michael conceived vehicles alone, and others when they were suggested and described in detail by the writers and then discussed with the model makers.

International Rescue's principal fire-extinguisher is the Firefly whose chief skill is to enter the very heart of the blaze and let loose nitro-glycerine shells which cause a blow-out. The nozzle that fires the shells pokes through a heavy-duty plate which can be raised to allow the nozzle a more flexible firing angle. Brain's supermetal, Cahelium Extract X, which was

Thunderbird 2 releases the pod containing Thunderbird 4 into the ocean (right). The front trap opens and the craft moves forward into the sea.

used in the construction of Fireball XL5, can resist the most blistering temperatures and forms the basis of the plate. Just like a giant bulldozer, the plate can shove interfering debris to one side. In 'City of Fire', the Firefly holds the blaze in check, while its plate clears the way so that the Mole can burrow its way to the trapped individuals.

Domo 1 is a brutish demolition machine, which can also move bulky objects from its path; it conceals a powerful nuclear reactor in its rear which powers three linked arms that can exert 64,000 pounds of pressure on any unfortunate object. In order to protect the operator from falling skyscrapers and collapsing mountain-sides, twelve-inch Formula C30/1 has been used for the cabin, with windows made out of nine-inch Visiglaze. Each arm ends in a large suction cup which contains an artificial gravity-field; this enables each cup to glue itself rigidly to any surface. With nuclear reactor going off at full tilt, and supersuction cups firmly in place, Domo 1 has no trouble in dispensing with objects of up to fifty tons.

With such entertaining gadgetry in tow, it is a pity that Domo 1 is only ever seen once when, in 'The Duchess Assignment', it supports a wall that is about to collapse, thus aiding the Mole to reach the cellar below.

Travelling on tracks, like most of the vehicles, to enable it to cope with rough terrain, the IR3 Transmitter Truck displays a giant dish which squats on its rear. The dish emits a beam to any spacecraft in distress and thus immediately assumes complete control of the shaky craft. A great asset in space rescues, IR3 has, like Domo 1, only been seen once in 'Sun Probe'. IR3 here saves Thunderbird 3 during a dual attempt to fire Sun Probe's retro-rockets.

Usually operated by Virgil, the aptly named Thunderiser is essentially a blaster gun that can get rid of bulky objects and slice through doorways. Electrical discharges which are more powerful than lightning enable a cutting laser beam to carve its way quickly to the heart of the rescue. In 'Thirty Minutes after Noon' it frees a British agent from a nuclear plutonium store, while a modified version fires up a rescue pack to the controllers of a television relay tower in 'The Edge of Impact'.

Fitted with eight wheels and caterpillar tracks, the Neutralising Equipment, which can defuse any ticking time-bomb, is operated by Brains. It makes its single appearance in 'Move and You're Dead', when Alan and Grandma are trapped on the San Miguel Bridge where, if either of them moves an inch, a bomb left by rival racing driver Victor Gomez will go off.

The Mobile Crane is possessed of a useful telescopic arm which can extend forty or fifty feet upwards. This it does in 'Path of Destruction', where Virgil and Brains are pushed skywards to rescue the crew of a Crablogger machine which has gone haywire. This was one instance where the machine involved could not be saved, thus embracing Jeff's message of humanity over machines.

The Elevator Cars, which feature dramatically in 'Trapped in the Sky', each have six sets of double wheels and a strong suspension platform to enable sticken aircraft to land on them without recourse to the undercarriage.

Employed in 'The Edge of Impact' and 'Pit of Peril', the remote television camera, which is carried inside a hatch on Thunderbird 1, is like a tiny aircraft which can cover difficult areas that Scott cannot see. It flies out of the hatch at speed to take up the necessary position.

In 'Pit of Peril', the Sidewinder is pulled from a pit by international Rescue's Recovery Vehicles which, by means of steel cables and two large suction missiles, can effect the task in hand. Just as useful is the Hover Bed which, operated by Virgil, emerges from Pod 1 to float on a bed of air on to which a person marooned above can jump with safety. See 'Move and You're Dead' for further details.

Like the Jetmobiles of 'Fireball XL5', the Hover Scooters, a tidy means of transport, are highly flexible ground vehicles. With seat and controls atop the fuselage, they travel down underground corridors in 'City of Fire' and also escape giant alligators in 'Attack of the Alligators'.

Resembling a vast and amusing carnivorous animal in its function, the Excavator, as seen in 'Martian Invasion', eats into impeding rocks and debris which, once clear of its digestive system, emerge via two chutes at the rear as dust and pebbles.

Powered by a radical new fuel called Superon, the Crablogger is more useful than the Junglecat in that, though it yanks trees from the ground, it also processes the wood in the back and offloads neat pieces onto a truck behind. The saws and grabs, meanwhile, adorn the front of a machine which is normally employed to clear the way for new roads.

The crew of the sabotaged Fireflash is picked up from the sea in Thunderbird 2's rescue arm as another mission is successfully completed.

THRILLS AND GASPS IN EVERY EPISODE

 'Trapped in the Sky'

Endangered by the Hood, who has planted a bomb in its bowels, the superplane Fireflash has to ignore its undercarriage and land instead on three radio-controlled Elevator Cars so the bomb does not explode. Fleeing the airport with photographs of Thunderbird 1, the Hood is hunted down by Lady Penelope on the M1 motorway.

 'Pit of Peril'

An American army spider-like Sidewinder crashes down into an old landfall which has been transformed into a raging inferno by combustible gases. Even International Rescue, with its state-of-the-art apparatus, has difficulty in winching it up.

 'City of Fire'

A car crash causes a blaze in an underground carpark and traps a family in the basement of the vast Thompson Tower. Burning rubble thwarts the rescue attempt of Scott and Virgil, who are now forced to use Brains's experimental gas which caused them to pass out during tests.

 'Sun Probe'

Three astronauts go into orbit to capture a piece of the sun but, when their retro-rockets fail, find themselves on a collision course instead. Thunderbird 3's own retros also fail during the rescue attempt; while, to add even more melo-drama to one of the most edge-of-the-sofa episodes, Thunderbird 2 has to endure a whirl-wind snowstorm.

 'The Uninvited'

Like the Hood, the malevolent Zombites operate from a secret temple and here shoot down Scott in Thunderbird 1. He is rescued by two archae-ologists who, after being captured themselves by the Zombites, are sprung to safety by Scott.

 'The Mighty Atom'

The Hood intends to wipe Australia off the map with a nuclear blast but is foiled by the wind, which keeps the radioactive cloud away from densely populated areas. He next causes another fire to draw International Rescue towards his trap; with the help on the Mighty Atom, a mouse-style robot which takes photographs with its eyes, he hopes to film Thunderbird 2 in

rewarding detail. He does not, however, reckon on the presence of Lady Penelope.

'Vault of Death'

Lord Sefton is finally convinced by Lady Penelope and Parker to modernise the Bank of England's main vault. Unfortunately, once the task has been completed, a hapless employee called Lambert is locked inside. While Penelope, Parker and Sefton rush to the bank in FAB 1, International Rescue overcomes the fact that Sefton has forgotten the key by tunnelling in via a disused underground railway line.

In their rear-mounted cockpit the crew of the Fireflash (above) looks out along the length of the atomic airliner on its maiden flight in 'Trapped in the Sky'. In 'Vault of Death' Parker demonstrates his safe-cracking skills (below).

THRILLS AND GASPS IN EVERY EPISODE

'Operation Crash Dive'

A Fireflash superplane is in trouble once again when it crashes into the sea, from which it is rescued by Thunderbird 4. Scott agrees to co-pilot the next test and, with no mechanical failure located, the plane once again plummets seawards. It is Gordon, winched aboard from Thunderbird 2, who discovers a violent saboteur.

'Move and You're Dead'

Hated by rival Victor Gomez when he announces his return to racing, Alan finds himself marooned with Grandma on a lonely Californian mountain bridge, which Gomez' bomb will destroy on detecting the slightest move. If they collapse in the heat, the bomb will surely explode. Will the ever-inventive Brains save the wilting twosome?

'Martian Invasion'

The Hood, anxious to deliver details of Thunderbirds 1 and 2 to the enigmatic General Strond, films both craft on a movie set when they arrive to save two actors who, dressed as Martians, are stuck in a cave.

'Brink of Disaster'

Pitting global con-man Warren Grafton against the ever-angelic Jeff, who feigns interest in Grafton's rip-off monorail scheme, this episode sends Jeff, Brains and Tin-Tin travelling on a dodgy monorail towards the jaws of a vast canyon. A faulty rail, brought about by Grafton's negligence, causes a disaster. Thunderbirds 1 and 2 come to the rescue, and Grafton is eventually brought to justice.

In 'Martian Invasion' Scott and Virgil are guests of a production crew filming the latest Martian science fiction epic. Could this be the successor to 'Thunderbirds'?

 12 ## 'The Perils of Penelope'

Seeking out Professor Borender, the inventor of a formula which converts sea-water into fuel, Lady Penelope and her friend Sir Jeremy Hodge are threatened in Paris and on a monorail train by Dr Godber. To prise Borender's secret from him, Godber places Penelope in the path of a speeding express train.

 13 ## 'Terror in New York City'

With mid-town Manhattan now indescribably shabby, an attempt is made to move the Empire State Building to pastures clean. It fails, and keen television reporter Ned Cook and his cameramen are thrown underground where they are trapped in a rapidly flooding cavern. With Thunderbird 2 inadvertently shot down by a navy warship, will Thunderbird 4 reach the site in time?

 14 ## 'End of the Road'

Constructing a road through a tropical rainforest, Eddie Houseman, a friend of the Tracys, is thwarted by landslides and so makes a determinedly crazy bid to save the project. He ends up teetering on a cliff-edge in his truck, so the Tracys must approach with caution while also keeping their identity from their friend Eddie.

 15 ## 'Day of Disaster'

A rocket is being transported to its launch site but, crossing a bridge which has been weakened by a storm, it plummets into the river and, with two engineers aboard, activates its own countdown mechanism. Thunderbird 4 must break through the rubble in time.

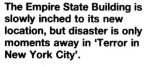

The Empire State Building is slowly inched to its new location, but disaster is only moments away in 'Terror in New York City'.

THRILLS AND GASPS IN EVERY EPISODE

16 'The Edge of Impact'

When General Bron asks him to sabotage the Red Arrow aircraft tests, the Hood cunningly causes a collision between a Red Arrow plane and a tele-relay tower. The tower sways in the breeze, and International Rescue must save the two men trapped above.

17 'Desperate Intruder'

Travelling to Lake Anasta in the Sahara Desert to locate a submerged temple and its buried treasure, Brains and Tin-Tin have to contend with the Hood, who wants not only the treasure but also access to International Rescue through the twosome.

18 '30 Minutes after Noon'

Britain's nuclear plutonium store is under threat of destruction by a marauding pack of vicious criminals whose files have been destroyed by fire at the Hudson Building in Spoke City. The gang is thwarted, and a vast nuclear explosion prevented, by the keen assistance provided by Lady Penelope.

19 'The Imposters'

A gang of criminals, in order to steal papers from an underground vault, stage a fake rescue mission under the convincing guise of International Rescue. An international hunt now begins to discover the Tracys' secret base. Despite being framed, however, they do need to save an astronaut who is floating free in outer space.

20 'The Man from MI5'

Under the guise of a top fashion model, Lady Penelope sails to the French Riviera in FAB 2 to help the British secret service recover plans for a nuclear device. She is promptly thrown into a boathouse with a time-bomb ticking away at her feet.

21 'Cry Wolf'

Two young Australian brothers inadvertently call Thunderbird 1 out on a mission by fooling around on their two-way radios. They are, moreover, soon in genuine trouble when the Hood, discovering that their father's weather station is really a space tracking station, traps the boys in an old mine. Will International Rescue take this next call seriously?

22 'Danger at Ocean Deep'

The mysterious disappearance of Ocean Pioneer 1 means that its special cargo of liquid alsterene will explode if it mixes with OD60, a chemical to be found in the sea where the ship vanished. Ocean Pioneer 2 is now travelling the same route with the same cargo.

23 'The Duchess Assignment'

The Duchess of Royston, an old friend of Lady Penelope's, has gambled her money away and so, with the help of Penelope, hopes to create income from renting out a valuable painting. Crooks soon lock her in an old house which then catches fire.

24 'Attack of the Alligators'

A boatman steals a wonderdrug which can cause animals to grow to four times their normal size. He drops some in the Amazon, and giant alligators launch an attack on the beleaguered lab.

One of Tin-Tin's holiday snaps (right) shows Lady Penelope riding by means of quite different transport in the film *Thunderbirds Are Go!*.

In 'Security Hazard' (below) Chip is returned safely to his bed to remember only the most wonderful dream after a visit to Tracy Island.

Playing at International Rescue can lead to disastrous consequences, as this little boy and his brother discovered in the episode 'Cry Wolf'.

Lady Penelope, aka Wanda Lamour, sings 'That Dangerous Game' accompanied by the Cass Carnaby Five. Lady Penelope at her best!

 'The Cham Cham'

The Cass Carnaby Five amusingly cause attacks on American space flights every time they perform their number 1 record. Discovering that the group's arranger is up to no good, Lady Penelope and Tin-Tin are soon endangered by a sabotaged cable-car.

 'Security Hazard'

An episode which is entirely free of stricken buildings, rampaging fires and bombed bridges, except in flashback, this homes in on a young stowaway who has been found aboard Thunderbird 2. Despite the Tracys' penchant for secrecy, he is treated to a nostalgic canter through the Thunderbirds missions. He falls asleep, awakes at home the next morning and wonders if it was all a dream.

27 'Atlantic Inferno'

With Jeff on holiday on Lady Penelope's Australian ranch, Scott is in charge and has to tackle a nuclear fire which erupts in the ocean near the Seascape oil-rig. The rig is engulfed by fire, as are two men who are trapped underneath in a bathysphere.

 ### 28 'Path of Destruction'

With its crew having fainted from food poisoning, a hulking Crablogger is heading dangerously towards the town of San Martino and a nearby dam. While Lady Penelope attempts to track down the designer, Brains and Virgil must board the rolling metal beast.

 ### 29 'Alias Mr Hackenbacker'

Brains, under the guise of Hiram K. Hackenbacker, joins forces with Lady Penelope when the new Skythrust airliner, which plays host to both Brains's new safety device and Lady Penelope's fashion show, is hijacked by a steward and one of the models who yearn for the secret of a new fabric, reverentially called Penelon.

 ### 30 'Lord's Parker's 'Oliday'

The first place to be powered by solar energy, Monte Bianco, may soon frazzle in the sun after the solar reflector collapses and beams malevolently down on the town. Penelope takes FAB 1 out to sea so as to send a distress call, while Parker and Bruno, the hotel manager, divert the residents from panic by offering homespun entertainment.

 ### 31 'Richochet'

A pirate radio station up in space is sent on a downward spiral by a renegade rocket. A malfunctioning Thunderbird 5 almost misses the distress call, disc jockey Rick O'Shea is afraid to be rescued and Virgil must stop the plummeting radio station colliding with a desert refinery.

 ### 32 'Give or Take a Million'

A New York toy shop is abused by criminals, who are trying to break into the bank next door. Escaping the police, they are finally trapped in a rocket which is ferrying Christmas presents to a children's hospital. The reward for their capture builds a new hospital wing, while one thrilled kid spends his Christmas break on Tracy Island.

The Seascape oil rig faces imminent danger as the World Navy testing of a new rocket goes disastrously wrong in 'Atlantic Inferno'.

BEFORE LIFT-OFF

In an era when big-screen action-thrillers have embraced a seemingly endless conveyor belt of special effects as the norm and, at their worst, have placed imagination on the back burner in so doing, it is heartening to home in on a television series which enthrals a world public.

Still Gerry Anderson's most accomplished creation to date, 'Thunderbirds' not only invented a wealth of special effects in order to realise the far-reaching scripts, but also never swamped credible story-lines, intriguing characters and exhilarating feats of daring with Thunderbirds 1–5 and an arsenal of heavy-duty machinery.

Thunderbird 2 surveys the danger zone around Seascape. Can the cracks in the sea-bed be safely capped?

'Thunderbirds' at once joined the front ranks as a bold vigorous experiment which even now has a sizeable audience of diehards. On 30 September 1965, for an eager audience in Great Britain, Thunderbirds were definitely go, and again in September 1991 for a new BBC2 audience.

Though 'Thunderbirds' creator Gerry Anderson has devised many puppet-based series since his early outings with 'The Adventures of Twizzle' and 'Torchy the Battery Boy', Gerry himself has often claimed that 'Thunderbirds' was the highlight of his career.

It was in fact, cigar-chomping British television mogul Lew Grade who insisted that Gerry make a new series to maintain the audience thrill after thirty-nine successful episodes of 'Stingray'. In the way that newspaper stories often give birth to novels, plays and feature films, Gerry was struck by a German mining disaster of the period and so began thinking about an international rescue team which would rush to the catastrophe but only when conventional methods had failed. Last-minute drama was thus inscribed on every episode.

Yet it was Lew Grade's spontaneous enthusiasm for the pilot episode, 'Trapped in the Sky', which quickly led to a clutch of initial problems. Working by his well-honed instincts, Grade felt that half an hour of space-age thrills was not enough and instantly decreed that each programme was to be one hour long. By the time he saw the pilot and let his exuberance fly, nine entire episodes had been shot, and a further ten scripts written, so Gerry was pleased by Grade's decision yet aware of the complications.

The team was committed to shooting a few more half-hours even after the thunderclap decision, while even later scripts were stretched to make up the full hour. Previously shot half-hours had to be doubled in length, while models which had already been destroyed, since they were deemed unnecessary for future programmes, had to be hastily rebuilt from scratch.

After so many shot nerves and sleepless nights, the final irony of this frenzied escapade – that the Americans finally decided to screen each episode in two half-hour segments – must seem amusing to Gerry and his team only in retrospect. This also meant extra work, since each second half had to be prefaced by a 'story so far'

synopsis. Yet their episode-stretching endeavours may well account for the continuing appeal of the series. Extending already filmed episodes like 'The Perils of Penelope' and 'Terror in New York City' inevitably led to a great deal more detail in both character and situation than in any other Anderson series, with the possible exception of 'UFO', which did not emerge until 1970. Viewers thus find it easier to grasp character motivation, empathise with the characters themselves and feel at home on Tracy Island. While Derek Meddings's intoxicating effects and often surreal rescue vehicles would lift the viewer, they would never dwarf the plain humanity of each situation.

Thunderbird 1 lands at a rescue site.

57

Thus, with a slot which followed straight after children's hour, Gerry and his wife Sylvia (who wrote the first script and kept an eye on the various commissioned writers) proceeded to produce at a rate of knots.

Sylvia Anderson's lively imagination ensured constant creative input. She was responsible for character visualisation and paid a great deal of attention to the appearance and sound of each puppet. John Tracy, for example, was initially cast as the dashing hero but, unhappy with his final appearance, Sylvia let Scott fill the lead role instead.

Sylvia decided on individual voices after the completion of each puppet. She provided the voice for Lady Penelope who was conceived by the puppet team with Sylvia in mind.

Born into a poor London family, and with no career plan in mind except a desire to become an architect one day, Gerry emerged from the London Blitz to attend Willesden Polytechnic. Discovering that he was not very gifted at the necessary architectural skill of technical drawing, he fortunately proved dexterous on the practical side and excelled in particular in the plaster shop. Only the film studios had any regular need for skilled plasterers, so he drifted towards the big screen through necessity rather than through any major obsession with film.

Yet Gerry became hooked on film after plaster became his enemy. Taking an examination which involved constructing a sizeable plaster piece, he ran out of plaster and so, mixing some up at great speed, he immediately encased his arm in it. When the plaster was removed, Gerry, owing to the lime in the plaster, lost the skin on both arms right up to the elbow and so developed lasting dermatitis. Strongly advised to move away from a career in plaster, Gerry was by now determined to work in the film business and so, after a period in the plaster shop of Gainsborough Pictures, he headed towards the Ministry of Information.

Gerry eventually secured a job through the Ministry of Information at the Colonial Film Unit which produced newsreels for Africa. This is when the puppet master really cut his teeth. Through spending six-week turns on both switchboard and projector, he also did identical-length stints on camera crew and film editing. It was

schoolmaster-turned-director George Pearson, one of the leading lights of British silent cinema, who pointed Gerry towards the cutting room, insisting that it would give the keen youngster an ideal grounding in all things film.

It was Gainsborough Pictures which gave Gerry his first proper break. Having completed shooting on *The Wicked Lady* (the most successful of the Gainsborough costume dramas),

Christmas at Creighton Manor.

befriended the series cameraman Arthur Povis. Homing in on all kinds of eccentrics, the series sent Gerry and Arthur to film a man who lived in a bottle for a year, to visit a lady who could write simultaneously in three languages scribbling with chalk in both hands, and to witness a fanatic who could propel himself on a bicycle at 109 miles per hour.

Many of Gerry's creative ventures sprang from AP Films, a company jointly launched by Gerry himself and Arthur Povis. They came upon a charming mansion by the Thames with a suitable flat to rent. Particularly keen on the fact that the mansion contained a small ballroom which they could transform into a handy film studio, they also turned the flat into an office and sat and waited, naïvely expecting that film and television moguls would order up films like pizza. With filing cabinet in the corner and notepaper on the desk, the phone was perpetually silent. They eventually ran out of money and so, trained technicians both, employed their skills to keep a non-active company afloat.

Gerry's emergence as a pioneering puppet guru had its origins in these unusual circumstances. Roberta Leigh was a writer who wanted to make a series of puppet films for the tiny budget of £450 a picture. Unsurprisingly spurned by the rest of the British film industry, which presumably could not take her seriously, she received a determined yes from Gerry and Arthur, to whom even £450 must have seemed a major handout from the gods. Gerry himself is even more emphatic: 'It was rather like a man finding a plank in the middle of the Atlantic. It's not the greatest find in the world, but when you're drowning it's a pretty good thing.'

These puppet films were Gerry's first major triumph as a director. 'The Adventures of Twizzle', fifty-two fifteen-minute films made between 1956 and 1957, concerned the antics of a boy doll who could extend both arms and legs and who inhabited Stray Town in the company of other lost toys. With Leigh producing, as well as writing scripts and songs, Gerry was firmly in charge as director.

He progressed both technically and in budget terms with his next series, 'Torchy the Battery Boy', which, as the title may suggest, was a more lavish rerun of 'Twizzle'. Concentrating on a

Gainsborough handed the picture over to an editorial team which included Gerry. The American distributors gasped in horror at Margaret Lockwood's low-cut dress. After taking out the offending close-ups, new footage was shot with Lockwood in a more puritanical state of cover-up.

Next directing a series which Anderson claims is of limited merit, 'You've Never Seen This', he dream paradise called Topsy Turvy Land, Torchy was another boy doll whose magic light lent him a special charisma. Feeling restless at piling invention upon invention in the service of someone else's show, Anderson and Povis decided to make their own programmes.

A huge success which was also translated into strip cartoon form in *TV Comic*, 'Four Feather Falls' took its cue from the popularity of the Western on screens both big and small and was laced with an appealingly lunatic surrealism.

Tex Tucker, sheriff of the town of the title, cares for the son of Indian chief Kalamakooya and so is given four magic feathers in return. While two feathers allow Tex's dog Dusty and his horse Rocky to speak, the other two galvanise Tex's six-shooter into rapid gunfire if the decent sheriff is boxed in by danger. While 'Carry On' regular Kenneth Connor voiced the quaint speech-patterns of both horse and dog, present-day game-show host Nicholas Parsons intoned the voice of Tex, while his wife Denise Bryer and Anderson stalwart David Graham (who later voiced Parker in 'Thunderbirds') supplied back-up.

More important in regard to 'Thunderbirds',

and the entire story of Supermarionation, 'Four Feather Falls' ushered in a new wave of technical expertise. The puppets were now controlled by much thinner wires which, carrying an electronic impulse to a solenoid in the head of the puppet, allowed them to open and shut their mouths in time to the prerecorded voices.

With Granada Television lending much-needed financial support to the series, and the problems of puppet realism preoccupying Gerry himself, he took one step nearer the puppet expertise of 'Thunderbirds' with his first space-age series, 'Supercar'.

At a time when science-fiction antics were replacing a waning interest in Westerns, and with Gerry's own admitted interest in aircraft and space travel in tow, he was primarily seeking a solution which would help his puppets walk convincingly from A to B. Though the puppets could pass muster as recognisable humans, their lumbering staccato walk often failed to submerge the viewer completely in a quirky fantasy world.

A set of high-speed wheels provided the answer. Reckoning that a special car which could propel the puppet cast on a series of adventures – be it on roads, in the air or under water – would

Mike Mercury and Professor Popkiss in their Nevada laboratory, Black Rock, with Supercar, 'the marvel of the age'.

mean that the puppets themselves would not actually have to give themselves away with too many gauche movements, Gerry was so pre-occupied with such technical details that he did not even consider it science fiction, in fact, in his own words, he did not even know what science fiction was.

Designed by Reg Hill (who would later re-emerge as associate producer on 'Thunderbirds') and Derek Meddings (supervising SFX director on 'Thunderbirds'), the Supercar itself, with its manifold abilities, was the star of all manner of high-drama escapades. Gerry's new expanded time-limit of thirty minutes per episode meant that plot-lines could be expanded, characters more fully developed and new characters introduced without any risk of cramming.

Aided generously by the puppet creators of the exhilarating super-machine, Professor Popkiss and his willing sidekick Doctor Beaker, the undeniable hero was Supercar pilot Mike Mercury, a man of such thrilling courage that even his name suggests he would have no trouble travelling at the speed of light. Lining up to help Mike were ten-year-old superkid Jimmy Gibson, who had himself been swept from trouble by the Supercar team in the first episode, and Mitch the Monkey who acted as a soft furry antidote to the gleaming hardware and twisted villains.

Chief among these was the mean-minded Masterspy who, much like the Hood in the later 'Thunderbirds', displayed an obsessive determination in his efforts to discover exactly what made Supercar tick.

With AP Films still not awash with money, they sank their entire funds into the 'Supercar' pilot before showing it to their previous backers, Granada, who, purely on budgetary grounds, turned it down flat. Enter television giant Lew Grade who, on a reduced budget, gave the green light for the entire thirty-nine episodes. Giving Gerry a giddy launch into the international market-place, especially the profitable American syndication market, in 1962, 'Supercar' was also notable as the first British television fantasy or science-fiction programme to concentrate on a piece of hardware.

Moving sideways to try his hand with the live-action television cop thriller 'Crossroads to Crime' (which concerns a young policeman who

Colonel Steve Zodiac, hero of *Fireball XL5* stands over uninvited guests in the control room of Space City.

pretends to take a bribe in order to lay a trap for some hijackers), as well as three prize-winning commercials for Blue Car Holidays, Anderson was soon requested by Lew Grade to follow the global impact of 'Supercar'.

'Fireball XL5', whose spirit of high adventure and constantly improving special effects gives a pointer to the advent of 'Thunderbirds', was the highly successful result. Featuring a more credible streamlined craft, which seemed a more likely contender for space travel than Supercar, and was also a tribute to the ever-expanding talents of Derek Meddings, the series replaced the schoolboy jokiness of 'Supercar' with fast-lane action thrills, though humour was still let in by the back door.

Chief space adventurer this time round was Steve Zodiac, whose fine-boned features were evidence of the continually improving Super-marionation techniques. He was joined in danger by the tempting Venus, whose come-on charisma took its lead from standard-issue Hollywood film stars with Professor Matthew 'Matt' Matic and Robert the Robot as decent support. Zoonie the Lazoon was a futuristic cousin of Mitch the

Monkey who balanced the hardware with cute childlike appeal.

With a name inspired by Castrol XL motor oil, and the craft's peculiar launch sequence that prefaced each episode devised by Gerry himself, Anderson also lent his presence to events on screen. Deciding that a strange disembodied voice was required for Robert the Robot, and denied the benefit of the digitally recorded sound of today, Gerry travelled to Edinburgh to investigate the development of an artificial larynx for people who had lost their voice through cancer. To activate the device, it had to be pressed firmly against the jaw, switched on and then words mouthed against its buzzing noise.

'Fireball XL5' became a huge favourite in America on Saturday morning television in 1963, while its theme song, sung by one Don Spencer, became a pop hit; the success of the series even spawned a rival, 'Space Patrol', created by former Anderson associates Roberta Leigh and Arthur Povis.

Yet it was 'Stingray' later that year that began the swell of Anderson-mania which would erupt soon afterwards with 'Thunderbirds'. The first British television series ever to be made in colour (thirty-nine episodes were produced from 1963 to 1964), it centred round the undersea heroics of James Garner look-alike Captain Troy Tempest of the World Aquanaut Security Patrol and his co-pilot George Lee Sheriden, more familiar as 'Phones'. More fully written characters were now appearing, with Commander Sam Shore, the head of WASP, and his daughter Atlanta providing a secure framework for Troy's watery feats. Ray Barrett lent his voice to Sam, while Atlanta's was provided by Lois Maxwell, alias Miss Moneypenny in the James Bond films. The evil Titan was in charge of the undersea tribes, and the mute Marina, whom Troy and Phones rescued from his grasp in the pilot episode, immediately became a useful member of the Stingray team.

With the American market in mind in particular, 'Stingray' was shot in colour (or Videocolor as the technique was called), yet was only able to be seen in Britain in black and white. Technical advances continued apace, so that bigger budgets meant more detailed sets (compare the beautifully crafted interior of Stingray with the spartan flight-deck of XL5), while the puppets themselves could now register a range of expressions. The smile, the frown and the in-between constituted the expressions available on a series of different heads.

Another feature, which became an established convention with 'Thunderbirds', was the inclusion of Christmas specials and flashback episodes. When a character announced, 'I remember when . . .', this took us back to an earlier adventure and also allowed Gerry himself to breathe temporarily in the midst of whirlwind deadlines.

It was at this time, too, January 1965, that *TV Century 21* (more affectionately known as *TV21*) was first produced and eventually became the most widely read British comic since the success of *Eagle*. Drawing upon the established expertise of editor Alan Fennell, who had written the majority of 'Fireball XLS' and 'Stingray' scripts, it was Anderson, who suggested the comic's newspaper format and the items of Twenty-First Century News on the inside. Gerry can still remember the edgy first few days before sales went into overdrive. Striking up conversation with his local newsagent, Gerry learned that of the seventy-eight copies he had bought in, only two sold on the first day, followed by one solitary copy on each of the following two days. Thereafter, it was as if every British child broke free of his or her restraining leash and bought up every copy in the land. *TV21* peaked with a colossal print run of 630,000. The regular imaginative treats in its pages, as well as the relative sophistication of 'Stingray', were moulding enthusiastic British youth in readiness for 'Thunderbirds'.

Alan Fennell, then editor of *TV21*, drew special attention to 'Thunderbirds' in issue 52 which went on sale in January 1966. Previously the assistant editor of *TV Comic*, Alan first met Gerry Anderson when negotiating a comic strip version of 'Four Feather Falls'. When he returned to do the same for 'Supercar' he was invited to write a 'Supercar' script. Alan emerged as a key scriptwriter for AP Films and wrote approximately half of all the scripts from 'Fireball XL5' through to 'Thunderbirds'.

Basking in the cosy warmth of universal success, the team set to work on two 'Thunderbirds' features, *Thunderbirds Are Go* (1966) and

Stingray, pride of the fleet of the World Aquanaut Security Patrol (WASP).

Thunderbird 6 (1967). Despite 'Thunderbirds' director, writer and script editor Alan Pattillo's slight reservation that 'the magic and intimacy of the small screen might be lost on the big', the first feature, in particular, was especially strong – yet both failed dismally at the box-office.

Lew Grade had immediately agreed to Gerry's suggestion of a first feature and to a budget of £250,000. Managers from the Rank Organisation attended a London preview of the film and gleefully cheered at key uplifting moments. How could it fail?

Despite being as convincing, thrilling, characterful and humanitarian as the television series, *Thunderbirds Are Go* took a spectacular nosedive at the box-office. A prime Christmas release-date and a national publicity tour, with Gerry himself as the main star, could not salvage the situation. Although the distributors told Gerry he had a James Bond on his hands in terms of commercial potential, Gerry would not become cash-happy at this stage but instead popped into local cinemas to witness his *Thunderbirds Are Go* entertaining audiences numbering only fifteen.

They were watching a film that exuded the same inventive spark, witty flair and oddball scenarios as the series itself. Multiple plotting, a sprinkling of monsters and a pop fantasy sequence including Cliff Richard and the Shadows (Cliff was once a neighbour of Gerry's in Portugal) were bolted on to the basic story of Zero X, which would propel man to Mars for the very first time.

Pilot Paul Travers, co-pilot Greg Martin and space navigator Brad Newman, as well as space scientists Dr Grant and Dr Pierce, are mastering the awesome technology of Zero X, the most advanced spaceship ever to leave a drawing-board. Glenn Field's understandable tension soon gives way to the spectacular launch of the massive steel hulk. Invisible to the crew, a furtive malcontent is strolling around the belly of the ship, happily taking photographs all the while. With his boot now trapped in the slick gadgetry of the ship, he winces in pain, pulls down his rubber mask and reveals himself as the Hood.

Having caused Zero X to plummet towards the ocean the favourite adversary parachutes clear of the craft, and the disappointed crew are subsequently recovered, thanks to International Rescue and an all-out quick-thinking rescue mission.

Although through this film 'Thunderbirds' enthralled a British audience in colour for the first time, many preferred to watch it in black and white at home. Confused as Gerry by the film's failure, United Artists at once commissioned another film to prove their resolve: *Thunderbird 6*. At least this film offers one comprehensible reason as to why it failed completely.

Teased into guessing the identity of the mysterious Thunderbird 6, the viewer is finally presented with a Tiger Moth as a witty gag. Unfortunately, a simple biplane could never compete with the knockout designs and abilities of Thunderbirds 1–5, while the big screen was an unsuitable place for the gentle irony of steam-age technology scoring triumphantly over an array of fantasy machines.

SUPERMARIONATION AND THE STRINGS BEHIND THE SPELL

A behind-the-scenes shot of the filming of 'Path of Destruction'. Note the attention to detail in the café setting.

All the Thunderbird puppets are still the key symbol of what was, in the mid-sixties, a radical new technique called Supermarionation. The process involved electronic control of realistic figures; yet, unlike the smoother electronic puppets of today, whose free-moving agility has replaced a sense of humanity, the process was not yet advanced enough to control the appealing staccato movements of arms and legs. Lips and eyes, however, did succeed in moving in a way which was marginally less quirky.

It is often wrongly assumed that, in comparison to modern electronic puppetry, Gerry was still a caveman in puppet terms; yet his technique was a breakthrough in its day. Before Gerry kick-started puppet technology and developed lip-sync, it was, for example, only possible to indicate that a puppet was speaking a line of dialogue by nodding its head up and down. Though some puppets of the pre-Anderson era had mouths which could open and close with a pull from the operator's string, their lips had an amusing tendency to develop a life of their own quite separate from the voiceover artist off-camera. Gerry's radical advance involved giving each puppet a flexible mouth and a pivoted tongue and lower lip which was connected to the chin by a flap of supple leather. A solenoid (a wire coil which carries an electro-magnetic field) connected to the puppet wires was secreted under the tongue. With the dialogue for each character carefully pre-recorded, it would then be transmitted to each puppet's wire by way of complex electronic gadgetry. The dialogue would then be played back and send off an immediate impulse which would open the mouth at the start of each word, while a return spring would shut it again at the end of the word.

By the time of Captain Scarlet technology was advancing apace and so the coils employed in the

New puppetry techniques were initiated during the filming of 'Thunderbirds'; these led to the type of animatronics that can be seen on the screen today.

Captain Scarlet and Blue are briefed by Colonel White aboard Spectrum's Cloudbase headquarters.

mouth movements were becoming ever smaller. It thus became possible to conceal the coil in the chest of the puppet, and consequently puppet heads shrank and became realistically proportionate to the body size. This new realism, though approaching perfection in one sense, ended the surrealism of large heads and tiny bodies which was a much-loved characteristic of 'Thunderbirds'. Paradoxically, the more accurate puppets now became, the more difficult it was to express their feelings and humanity.

The whole process of Supermarionation was unique to Gerry's company, AP Films. Shot in 35 mm colour, 'Thunderbirds' was filmed on complete film stages which were barely a fifth of live-action size. Subtle tricks included back projection and matching live-action drop-in shots with the kind of special effects which would be unthinkable in any standard-issue live-action movie. Gerry also had to grapple with

how to create a sense of depth on stages which, though only eight to ten feet deep, had to play host to often complex action sequences.

The puppets themselves dominated this new search for credibility for which due credit must be paid to Lew Grade and Associated Television, who dug deep to back this radical new process. Such expenditure had already frightened off the art-driven studios of France, Italy and West Germany and even the normally cash-happy moguls in Hollywood.

Christine Glanville, Gerry Anderson's chief puppeteer on 'Thunderbirds', reminisces with affection about puppets which were barely more than twenty-two inches tall: 'There were, you know, only three sizes of body. One size male body for all the boys and Jeff, a smaller body for Brains and Kyrano, and a standard-size female body.'

While the bodies were made by John Blundell,

Christine herself actually constructed the heads for Scott, Alan and Tin-Tin. Sharing puppet tasks with her co-puppeteer, Mary Turner (who created the wonderful Lady Penelope), both ladies would operate all the puppets since 'whichever floor puppeteer was on duty would bring them to the bridge, ready to start.'

Because neither Gerry nor his colleagues could draw, the proposed appearance of each

Tin-Tin and Lady Penelope share a friendly chat in the puppet store (below) as they wait to be called to the set.

Hours of work were spent on the detailed preparation before final production of the puppets' heads.

puppet was described in terms of real-life individuals. As Christine herself now explains:

'We had a copy of *Spotlight* [the directory which includes portrait photos of actors] and we would decide on types. Without reference to specific real-life individuals, it would have been hard for Gerry to get his ideas across. For example, Scott was modelled on Sean Connery, the handsome hero-type of the day. Alan looked like the son of a father-and-son lawyer team which was popular on television at the time, while Virgil looked like Alan. In fact Virgil was John Brown's first attempt at creating a puppet, and he ran into difficulties, so I said, "Why don't you copy Alan?", knowing that Virgil would emerge as John's version of Alan and therefore suitably different.'

John, in fact, went on to create Jeff Tracy who, in Christine's view, is one of the finest puppets in the series. Her particular favourite is Scott who, aside from the obvious fact that he was created by Christine, 'looked like James Bond and had lovely dimples'.

Although she believes any more puppet realism

Scott's hands operated the controls of Thunderbird 1 as his elbows were moved from behind by the puppeteers.

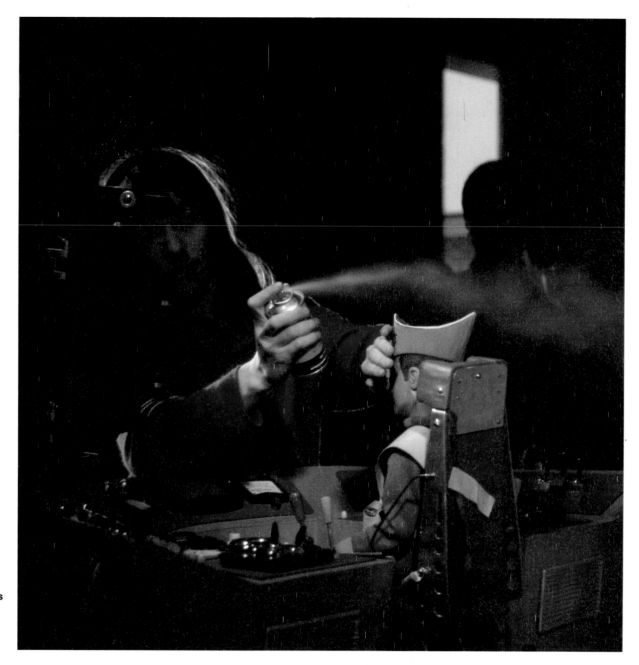

would have removed much of the heart, she stresses the need to accept the limitations of the puppet form: 'In a photograph puppets may look like real men, but it's clear they're not when they try to move.' The balance between realism and artifice was, she admits, about right.

It was the working of the puppets which Christine enjoyed most since she could really bring them to life. While her own puppet operations displayed a great deal of humanity, Mary Turner's, she believes, were more accurate. 'Thunderbirds' writer, script editor and director

Alan Pattillo voices an equal enthusiasm for both puppeteers, contrasting the more 'balletic, natural, graceful' style of Christine with the more angular, experimental interpretations of Mary:

'I remember one scene from "Fireball XL5" in which Venus is hypnotised by a planet outside the window. Christine was the puppeteer on Venus for the first take, and her version was typically graceful. But for some reason we had to do a retake and this time round used Mary. Her interpretation of Venus' reaction was much more strange and disturbing, but equally convincing.'

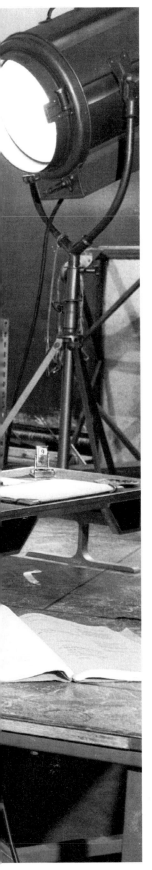

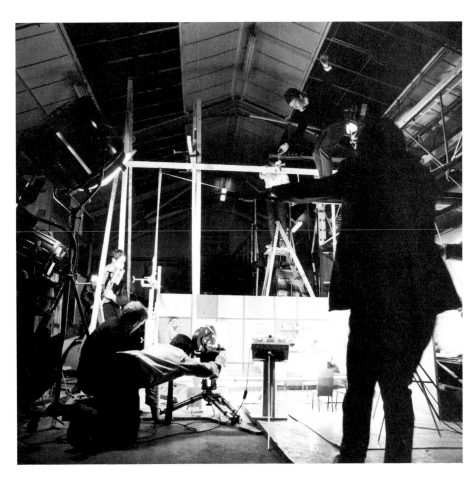

A demonstration of Scott's method of boarding Thunderbird 3 (left); the operator controls the sofa by means of a hydraulic jack beneath the platform.

Lights, camera, action! An excellent example of the film crew at work (right).

All puppets had interchangeable heads, each one of which revealed a different facial expression; yet they never once turned out the same despite being cast in the same mould and finished in exactly the same way. There was constant friendly rivalry between the two units to secure the best heads for their particular set of puppets. (In order to make the transmission deadlines, two units filmed simultaneously, without which each episode would have required four weeks to shoot.

Christine herself confirms the strangeness of one mould giving birth to different bodies and heads: 'Two puppets could share the same body, the same weight, the same hole for the neck and indeed the same neck, yet some would always work better than others. That's always been a mystery to me, even now.'

Still professionally active, Christine has just worked with Gerry on the recent Dire Straits video, *Calling Elvis*, in which puppet versions of band members would pass muster on Tracy Island, while she concocted 'luscious kissing lips

and sniffing noses' for a German detergent ad.

Long before she embarked on her first venture with Gerry in 'The Adventures of Twizzle', she had, when still a young girl, visited a puppet exhibition with her mother. Her mother became intrigued, began to make simple puppets, and consequently both her parents took puppetry up as a hobby. Her mother also became acquainted with someone who had a puppet theatre in Chiswick Mall in West London, and Christine began working there as an operator at weekends. Employing her puppet skills, too, at children's parties, Christine finally moved into variety and cabaret through which she was finally introduced to Gerry.

Despite a tight timetable, no attempt was made to take lazy short-cuts or to spare perfection. It was arduous enough in the first place just creating the puppet characters. Heads were sculpted in clay, then roughly painted so that the final result could be forecast. On a good day, the head would enter the next stage of the process, but more often than not it would be scrapped

and work would start from scratch once again. Heads which could match the proposed visualisation would then be copied in the form of a fibreglass shell.

Puppet bodies were always constructed in plastic and, because of simplification allowed by the three basic body sizes, could be produced in bulk at short notice. Weight, too, was often a problem because if, for example, the puppet was too heavy it would require thick control-wires which would strain the operator and be visible on screen; very light puppets, on the other hand, could not be controlled effectively.

After actual manufacture, puppets were next supplied with operating wires before being dangled from the twelve-foot-high gantry for testing. Even with its puppets fully dressed for work, there was still enough time to make minor adjustments to lip and eye movements. Any alteration could not be made lightly since, because of the constant need for an identical twin to feed the second unit which was working simultaneously, and discrepancy in facial detail, mould or paint finish would be picked up by a probing camera which was sensitive to every detail of a small-scale set.

'You rang, M'Lady?' (left)

In his temple deep within the Malaysian jungle the Hood plots to infiltrate the network of International Rescue.

Associate producer Reg Hill harks back to terms like 'smilers' and 'scowlers' which they applied to the four or five different heads for each puppet (eight or ten including the duplicate model), according to the prevailing expression on the face. In addition, special effects shooting required single puppets to be re-created to quite different scales.

The entire Tracy clan, as well as Lady Penelope, Parker, Brains, Kyrano and Tin-Tin, were constructed largely from fibreglass, while plastic was deemed sufficient for the so-called 'revamp' puppets which functioned in a cameo or support capacity. Parker, initially envisioned as Penelope's sidekick, soon occupied centre screen and thus made the flattering transition from plastic to fibreglass. Parker himself would undoubtedly have approved of such a promotion.

Taking a cue from the motor industry in its manufacture of glass-fibre car bodies, AP Films took delivery of polyester resin and a special glass-fibre cloth, the latter being judged as smooth enough for modelling. After a plastic mould was completed, the creator of the particular puppet began to laminate, laying on several resin-soaked layers of cloth. Dry to the touch in

A publicity shot of Alan Tracy.

thirty minutes, it was fully set in an hour, with a natural colour of beige and the resin completely translucent. Though a fire-resistant resin was available, there was, despite the use of mini-rockets, no special request for fireproof puppets. The puppets also benefited from a putty-like substance called Bondapaste, which was used to fill cracks and add contours, even though it was not designed with bonding in mind.

'Fireball XL5' and other Supermarionation adventures were peppered with coloured puppets, chiefly because of the difficulty in finding grey, white and black fabrics which matched the way the stories were visualised. Plasticine modelling also naturally led to coloured heads. But with 'Thunderbirds' now shot in 35 mm Eastman Kodak, perfect colour-matching was a must.

Typically, nine long wires would operate each twenty-two-inch puppet from a steel gantry twenty-five feet wide. The ever-expanding team of puppeteers (the quaint theatrical term used on set in preference to the official one, Super-marionators) would, after carrying out their share of puppet construction, split in two; at least six would work as manipulators, the others improving the 'revamps' and constructing additional characters.

The wires that moved many, but not all, of the 'Thunderbirds' puppets were only occasionally visible on screen, despite the many jokes made about them over the years. The odd unexpected guest appearance of a stray wire only ever added to the pleasurable gap between the attempted realism and gauche puppetry.

Yet this did not stop the 'Thunderbirds' team from regarding intrusive wires with horror. Associate producer Reg Hill confesses that wire always caused a headache since, in order both to support and to move the weight of a seven- or eight-pound puppet, a steel wire had to be 0.005 inches in diameter, although they could get away with 0.003 for the arms. Given that a standard human hair, which is around 0.002 inches, can often be distinguished on a decent television screen, much thought went into the problem of visible wires. Of other stronger alloys, only copper could be reduced to the required thinness; however, once it was stretched, it remained in that position. The capacity of wire to give off reflections was minimised in various ways, while

An operator prepares a puppet for filming.

The Hood's lair, from behind the camera.

in special-effects sequences, where cameras are often just feet away from the subjects, wires were often painted so as to blend in with the background.

Supervising special effects director Derek Meddings talks amusingly about the transition from television to features in terms of the wires. It was often suggested to Derek that, whereas wires were mostly invisible on the small screen, they would appear large on the big. He always replied to the film executives that he always showed them the rushes for each episode on a cinema screen at Pinewood and, with all wires highly visible, they had never once curled a lip or scoffed in disdain. Derek adds that, although he would blot out a wire that he could see on set, it would still sometimes be picked up by the camera. With a typical insistence on high production values, the team would reshoot an entire sequence whenever an uninvited wire strayed on to the screen. Only on odd occasions was it impossible to reshoot.

Yet moments of fun penetrated intense shooting schedules. Since all the puppets sported artificial human eyes, Gerry once contacted an eye-maker, who knew nothing of his puppet enterprises, to ask for a quote, and the specialist was suitably stunned when Gerry asked for the price of a pair.

A rolling road, in fact, along with a rolling sky was designed by supervising special effects Director Derek Meddings for 'Thunderbirds'. The road, which is still in active use in the Bond films, was employed in conjunction with a smaller road–sky moving model to create a convincing impression of speed. The effect can be seen to best advantage in 'Trapped in the Sky', when the disabled jet airliner comes in to land on three Elevator Cars.

Derek, who not only had a character named after him in the first episode, but also went on to take charge of the effects for the Bond films and *Batman*, can recall showing Gerry a drawing of Thunderbird 2 which bore no resemblance to the script. Much to Derek's surprise, Gerry loved Derek's invention of a giant green bug. Despite being the most difficult Thunderbird to fly, it eventually became Derek's own favourite, and its surreal beauty, which is grandiose and anarchic, has been much adored by artists like

Preparing to film a launch. Models of different sizes were made according to the shots required. This model of Thunderbird 3 was one of the largest craft made.

Frank Bellamy. Perversely, Derek made its wings point forward, so placing Thunderbird 2 amusingly at odds with the backward thrust of conventional high-speed craft. Unimpressed by the appearance of Thunderbird 3, Derek least favoured Thunderbird 1, which he found both ugly and dull to film, since it could only be shot from one limiting angle. He adds that Thunderbird 2's size made it difficult to fly, since it had to dwarf the rescue vehicles it was carrying. Had they been any smaller, then they would have been unable to function. This example aside, there was never any conscious attempt to build all the craft in proportion to one another, while the sequence where the sofa speeds through the base of Thunderbird 3 was the only time that Derek constructed a large-scale set-piece.

Of all the set creations, supervising art director Bob Bell's favourite was The Whistle Stop Inn, a station restaurant in *Thunderbird 6*, 'in which trains puff in and out and deliver food to the waiting customers'. He laughs as he admits that 'anything I was asked to do which was a bit dull, I'd pass on to someone else. It was all very hard work, because we had to build all the props from scratch and so create our own props store. It wasn't like a live-action film where you can hire everything.'

Continual fretting with regard to lighting, depth of focus, water scenes and fire was, despite the arm-twisting timetable for each episode, always resolved in some way. Having first toyed with the conventions of dry ice and chemical smoke for full rocket effect, it was then decided to use the real thing. Schermuly Pistol Rocket Apparatus Ltd, which designed Royal Naval and other life-saving rocket devices, dreamed up compressed gunpowder rockets for 'Thunderbirds'. Coupled with an increased camera speed, all jet motors, retro-rockets, explosions and rocket-launches became miniature versions of the real thing.

Running repairs were carried out on the vehicles during production. Here we see Thunderbird 2 receiving some minor attention (above).

Craft control wires also had to be concealed. Here the size of the smaller model of Thunderbird 3 emerging from the Round House can be compared with that on the opposite page.

One potential problem resolved itself in an entertaining way. For 'Attack of the Alligators', it was decided that, since there was no money in the budget to create miniature alligators, real baby crocodiles would be found which would be in scale with the series. Even though water-tanks were set up and heated to the correct temperature, he was paid a surprise visit by an RSPCA inspector who had been told that the crocodiles were being given nasty electric shocks. The inspector was promptly distracted when he realised that it was 'Thunderbirds', his favourite programme, which was being filmed, and after half an hour of wide-eyed enthusiasm he finally tackled Derek Meddings about the purpose of his visit. Because the crocodiles wouldn't move, Derek said, he had touched them with an electrode, to no avail. On learning that Derek was only using twenty volts, the inspector recommended, because of the animals' thick skins, a sixty-volt dose. The exuberant official ended up taking his annual leave to work for Gerry and so applied the electric shocks himself.

While the three-foot crocodiles were mainly functional, except for a particularly docile specimen which loafed all day on the studio floor, a five-foot animal was too vicious to remove from its basket. Derek himself had his own freaky moment when filming that episode. With a non-slip knot around a crocodile's neck, Derek had pulled that animal through and up from the water to make it look as if it was about to snap off the back of a boatful of people. However, for the next shot, where the beast had to open its mouth, Derek, still in the tank in his waders, pulled on the rope to find nothing there. The crocodile had freed itself, and Derek could detect a V-shape rippling through the water; he managed to jump up on to the edge of the tank, leaving his boots in the water.

Penelope (right) remains calm while posing for this publicity shot. Alligators are a girl's best friend!

A production shot of the Seascape oil rig from the episode 'Atlantic Inferno' (left).

Water effect shots had to be taken from the most difficult positions. Cameraman and camera were often balanced at precarious angles (above).

DAZZLING THE EARS AND THE EYES

The composer, arranger and conductor for both films, and indeed for the entire 'Thunderbirds' series, was Barry Gray, who sadly died in 1984 yet is remembered with genuine affection by Gerry and the entire team. A polite and gentle man, he was the musical force behind 'Thunderbirds' and thus a key contributor to the success of the series and Gerry's other early work. Chiefly known as the composer of the rousing 'Thunderbirds' march, which a generation of children would hum for years as they slid down banisters pretending to be Scott or Virgil, he was also responsible for the electronic effects which peppered the series.

Standing apart from the often banal world of television and film music, which regularly appears as an add-on or afterthought, Barry's music for 'Thunderbirds' was an integral part of the drama. Clearly in touch with the characters and their missions, and an obvious fan of the series himself, Barry was paid constant respect by the eighty orchestra members.

A man of small stature, Barry would have no trouble at all in establishing command. One tap of his baton was all that was needed for complete silence. Despite the mighty roar of the 'Thunderbirds' march during the filming of *Thunderbirds Are Go*, Barry would dazzle onlookers with his ability to single out a wrong note from the heat of the musical furnace.

Having made a deep study of the history of music, Barry could play any number of musical instruments and grasp any style of music with ease. Equally *au fait* with recording techniques, he had his own studio and always seemed relaxed and happy when surrounded by banks of state-of-the-art gadgetry.

Barry played a key role in the development of Gerry's own series. For both 'The Adventures of Twizzle' and 'Torchy the Battery Boy', Roberta Leigh, though often credited as composer, had hummed the music into a tape-recorder; and Barry had then arranged it. At this point in his life, Barry was purely an orchestrator and arranger; yet he would secure his first chance as composer with 'Four Feather Falls'.

Gerry, who had yet to attempt to write a script, or indeed create a programme, but was keen to break from Leigh and dream up his own series, told Barry of his intention to do just that. Barry himself was keen to think up an idea, and the result was 'Four Feather Falls', which pushed Gerry, via 'Supercar', 'Fireball XL5' and 'Stingray', towards 'Thunderbirds'. Though Barry made no financial gain from 'Four Feather Falls', he made a strong mark as a composer in his own right.

'Thunderbirds' director, writer and script editor Alan Pattillo has fond memories of Barry:

'So that we could edit, we'd often need a bit of music for our cutting copy. Barry would always be helpful, enthusiastic and creative and record something for us on his synthesiser. It was always fun to pay him a visit. He lived in a little house in Dollis Hill, a 1920s bungalow, with his mother. He had a small studio in the back room. He was also, you know, Vera Lynn's accompanist during the height of her wartime fame.'

**Thunderbird 2 piloted by
Virgil with Brains and
Gordon as crew.**

Despite a continuing successful worldwide career as a film editor, nothing is quite so 'nostalgia-inducing' in Alan's life as 'Thunderbirds' which allowed him to blossom effectively as writer, script editor and director. Through film editor David Elliott, who went on to direct many of the 'Thunderbirds' episodes, Alan met Gerry and was hired at once as an editor, before progressing to director several weeks later. He had, in fact, directed several episodes of 'Supercar', but it was on 'Thunderbirds' that he emerged as writer and script editor.

Pattillo, a pleasantly guarded man who combines precise analytical insights with Aberdonian charm, speaks fondly of his progress through the ranks:

'Everything mushroomed for Gerry so much that he wanted someone to take charge of all the scripts and deal with the other writers, too. So, about two months after we filmed the pilot, "Trapped in the Sky", I became the series script editor. I would discuss story-lines with Gerry and the required special effects with Derek Meddings.'

It seems there was never any problem with ensuring that key writers Alan Fennell and Dennis Spooner, as well as other contributors, were travelling down the same road. Story-lines would be worked out to a high degree and then the writers would meet Gerry and Alan for morning coffee or afternoon tea to discuss the scripts.

Lady Penelope relaxing on her Australian ranch.

82

AQUANAUT
THUNDERBIRD 4
GORDON TRACY

The opening caption shots of Lady Penelope and Gordon.

In his multiple roles, Alan was very concerned with the difficulties of puppet filming:

'It was difficult for puppets to get in and out of vehicles without a great deal of trouble. Since we always tried to minimise walking, we'd show the puppets taking one step only, then promptly cut. Through interspersing the programmes with "meanwhile" scenes – that is, showing what else was going on in the story at the same time – we would then cut back to the puppet who was by now already in his craft. But for "Trapped in the Sky" we went to an enormous amount of trouble to show puppets getting in and out of vehicles. These sequences, along with any spare takes, became stock shots which were used time and again.'

Confessing that 'while half of us were trying to make the puppets walk realistically, the other half had accepted that they were just puppets', Alan Pattillo believes that the jump-start walk, the shrugging shoulders and jerky head-movements added to the enormous appeal of the series. The 'Thunderbirds' characters were seen

Wayne Forrester and Paul Kent as Colonel White and Captain Scarlet.

as attractive enough by the team for the addition of a fetching animal, which had characterised 'Supercar' and 'Fireball XL5', and 'Stingray' (Marina had a pet seal called Oink), to be unnecessary.

Alan still holds much affection for a concept which dovetails technical gimmickry with obvious humanity:

'Now electronic puppets, though versatile, can be so cold that you may as well use real actors. It can all be a bit soulless. The family values, in which a father dispatched yet looked after his sons on their various missions, were a big part of our appeal. With all our characters carefully worked on, and with the support of good vocal artists, we had Gerry's best mix so far.'

Gerry, it seems, was excellent at not pressurising the team, despite their frantic two-week deadlines or, as Alan says 'he was good at being uninterfering, and not pushing it too far'. Sometimes, indeed, they even finished ahead of schedule.

Because he wanted to move on, Alan did not script-edit the final six programmes, though he contributed both 'Alias Mr Hackenbacker' and

'Give or Take a Million' as a writer. He declined Gerry's offer to stay on board for *Thunderbirds Are Go*, thinking 'it would be too much hassle on the big screen, with puppet wires showing'. Yet Alan looks back on these years of committed fun with a resonant glow which causes him to discuss single programmes as if they were made yesterday.

It is the limitations of the puppet form which largely contribute to the charisma of *Thunderbirds FAB*, a stage show which is an affectionate parody of Gerry Anderson's creation and has charmed audiences the world over since it began life in 1985 as a small-scale touring production.

In 1989 the show really lifted off. At a time when Batman ruled the world and more than sixty comic-book projects were being put together for both big and small screens, it was unsurprising that two well-known English actors, Andrew Dawson and Gavin Robertson, brought Gerry Anderson's *Thunderbirds FAB* to a West End stage. Once the fodder of dingy pub theatres, the two young men benefited from a soaring interest in comic books and were thus catapulted into the

West End itself. The show, in fact, broke all house records at the Apollo Theatre, London.

Gavin Robertson is still modestly reeling from the shock that the success of *Thunderbirds FAB* has been so colossal: 'We stumbled on "Thunderbirds" in complete naïvety and conceived of it as only a little part of a much bigger show. At Lecoq School in Paris, as well as the Desmond Jones School of Mime, Andy and I had learned the archetypal mime movements of classic marionettes, but we now had to analyse what made the "Thunderbirds" puppets move. It was particularly tough teaching this to the new actors!'

A fan of Lady Penelope in particular ('everyone's waiting for her, and we would be surprised if she didn't appear'), Gavin explains: 'Originally the craft were to be perched on our shoulders,

but we figured they'd be too small to be seen at the back of the theatre, so we then decided to wear them like huge hats.'

Both a tribute to and a parody of the mid-sixties hit television series, the production was an imaginative showcase for the two talents who delighted both themselves and the audience with those wonderfully staccato limb-movements that have you straining in the dark for giveaway strings. At times, and admirably faithful to the television originals, their hands would dangle pointlessly in mid-air.

A canny mix of schoolboy innocence and arty shrewdness, Dawson was excellent as Scott Tracy, the keen-minded captain of Thunderbird 1, while Robertson was equally adapt as the hapless Virgil living in the shadow of his brother and only allowed to pilot Thunderbird 2. When not acting out the cockpit antics of the two superheroes, both artists were able to stage spectacular nose-dives and heady acts of lunacy with only a few deft hand-movements and some telling squints of the face. Dawson's face, in particular, looked as if it were being pulled in all directions at once by invisible fingers.

Precision timing, simple lighting and elements of pantomime also enabled Robertson to turn Lady Penelope into an exercise in camp, while Dawson's sprawling limbs were ideal for his version of Captain Scarlet. The spoof was completed when both actors reappeared to let Thunderbirds 1 and 2 take the stage as fetching headgear.

A more solemn Space Panorama, which served as an opening act to the show, was designed as an affectionate satire of Neil Armstrong and chums landing on the moon. Noisy levity and quiet melodrama both found their place in a piece which parodied both bland news-speak and our uncritical devotion to technology.

The recent version of the stage show, which last year returned to London's theatreland in celebratory style, was now directed by its creators, Gavin Robertson and Andrew Dawson. Actors Paul Kent and Wayne Forester were in the cockpit this time round and amusingly fleshed out twelve Anderson creations, including Scott and Virgil Tracy, Brains, Parker and Lady Penelope. Any casual theatregoer who had never immersed himself in the specialist universe of the 'Thunderbirds' fan would blink twice before grasping that mirror-image versions of the characters on stage were liberally sprinkled throughout the auditorium.

Wayne and Paul perform a spectacular launch sequence during their performance of *Thunderbirds FAB: the Next Generation*.

SPELL UNBROKEN

Certainly 'Thunderbirds' has sparked the imagination of a world public like no other puppet series before or since. Yet its influence, extending beyond millions of eager viewers, has also been both technical and ideological.

Back in the mid-sixties, an established British film studio was facing problems as it grappled with the task of filming a live-action air crash in open countryside. For three weeks they strived to squeeze credibility from a balsa-wood model crashing on to pylon wires. Unhappy with the resulting lame effect, they requested assistance from AP Films and, having seen AP's own crashing sequence for 'Thunderbirds', had their own shot in the can in just one afternoon.

Amongst all the rumours about the influence of 'Thunderbirds', Gerry himself believes that, although it may not be true that American air force designers were inspired by the series, it did excite a future generation of scientists and engineers, whose ideas have been shaped by the craft and their capabilities. Meanwhile, charities and the Government (through their public safety films) have often employed International Rescue. And thus the dynamism of the characters, the breezy confidence with which they reacted and the ease with which they handled their freshly minted machinery drew a deceptive cloak over the full-tilt effort which Anderson and many others lavished on this complicated series.

Still creating ever more inventive rescue operations, Gerry had intended to go out on a high after the first exhilarating batch of twenty-six

GERRY ANDERSON'S
Thunderbirds

episodes and move on to a new project, most likely with Zero X as the starring machine. However, the enthusiastic support from his world-wide public led to a further six episodes, which were first broadcast in autumn 1966.

To the avid 'Thunderbirds' *aficionado*, the final six programmes were markedly different, even though only a handful of small details tilt the scales. 'Atlantic Inferno', 'Path of Destruc-

A selection from a set of 'Thunderbirds' postcards produced in recent years by Engale Marketing in Blackpool. Complete collectors' sets (of which there are three) are now quite rare.

tion', 'Alias Mr Hackenbacker', 'Lord Parker's 'Oliday', 'Ricochet' and 'Give or Take a Million', constitute the six shows.

Like the twenty-six previous shows, each episode cost around £22,000 (roughly what Anderson's more recent 'Terrahawks' cost in equivalent terms). Keen eyes will pick up on the fact that, in the final six, the Thunderbirds logo carries the date 1966 instead of 1964, while the puppets themselves, all of which edge away from caricature and move towards realism, sport an array of minor, and barely perceptible, differences. The only vocal difference was that David Holliday, who originally supplied the tones of Virgil Tracy, was not available in time, so Jeremy Wilkin replaced him.

Despite our ability now to view the 'Thunderbirds' series in colour, in Britain it was only possible to watch the programmes initially in black and white, though Gerry had made the entire series, like 'Stingray' before it, in a splash of wonderfully contrasting colours. For quite some years, British fans could only enjoy the brightly coloured craft on the big screen and through the popular pages of *TV21*.

The most recent ideological impact of 'Thunderbirds' led to the creation of a real-life International Rescue in the early-eighties: a team of roughly seventy highly skilled operational volunteers which flies in, courtesy of free British Airways seats, to the scene of a disaster. In the manner of Scott Tracy, but with staccato body-movements nowhere in sight, they arrive at the zone with talking rope, thermal-imaging cameras and other pieces of advanced rescue equipment, pinpoint the requirements and move on quickly to the next spot. The honorary president of International Rescue Corps, by the way, is Gerry Anderson himself.

Gerry has thought at times of reviving his International Rescue as a live-action show or a new puppet production, while allowing himself to change a number of details. Lady Penelope, who would now drive a Porsche, would also, as a concession to the times, have given up smoking; while Brains would be relieved of his thick-lensed glasses and Scott of his simple Boy Scout persona. Though this has never occurred, the series has recently been repeated on BBC2 in its thirty-two component parts to over six million

(Opposite) From left to right: Reg Hill, Sylvia and Gerry Anderson and John Read at the Slough Studio at the height of 'Thunderbirds' original success.

A publicity shot (above) of Lady Penelope and Jeff reading a preview copy of the novelisation of their adventure *Thunderbirds are Go!*.

viewers, while 'Thunderbirds 2086', a Japanese television cartoon series with new characters and craft, (and no connection with Gerry Anderson) has recently been relaunched on video. The affectionate parody of the original series, *Thunderbirds FAB: The Next Generation* continues to attract theatre crowds and Thunderbirds fans across the world.

One such 'Thunderbirds' devotee is Lorraine Malby, a twenty-eight-year-old East Ender whose chief fancy is dressing up like Virgil Tracy. A ten-inch yellow sash and seemingly shrunken peaked cap sit strangely on an otherwise respectable insurance clerk. It calls to mind Clark Kent, who, gauche, bespectacled grey suit in his day job, would vanish into a callbox and re-emerge only moments later as Superman.

Unusual in that she has a tolerant mother who sees nothing odd in all this, Lorraine confesses that: 'My mum understands, because she's a Trekkie, but Dad can't understand it. He's into model railways, you see.' Lorraine even bought her mother a blue uniform which is a quality match for Mr Spock's in *Star Trek*.

Ralph Titterton, who is in charge of merchandising and liaison for Fanderson (the Gerry Anderson appreciation society), is clearly in no danger of becoming Scott Tracy. Initiating a range of products which are available exclusively to Fanderson members, he has been 'totally hooked throughout the years' since he first saw 'Fireball XL5' in 1961. Despite his avid worship of all things Anderson, and impressive rooms full of neatly stacked books and videos, as well as assorted rare memorabilia, he realises he is not living in 2026 but in present-day Ashford, Kent: 'For certain fans, "Thunderbirds" has become a religion, yet I've never lost sight of the fact that it's just a television programme, albeit an excellent one, made to make money for its backers.'

A charge nurse at an intensive and coronary care unit in Dover, he shares both his house and his enthusiasm, the reasons for which he finds 'difficult to describe', with his girlfriend Cathy Ford to whom he presented a raffle prize at a Fanderson convention long before they became co-pilots. Combining an open-hearted delight in Gerry Anderson's puppet universe with a charming ability to smile wryly at their joint fascination, they are unlikely to emulate the

Any Thunderbirds collector would be envious of this display of original 1960s merchandise.

Tracy brothers' staccato puppet walk as they stroll round the town of Ashford.

The products offshoots of 'Thunderbirds' were tremendously varied. Alan Fennell was assisted in the creation of *TV21* by Keith Shackleton, managing director of AP Films Merchandising, which, in early 1966, went on to become Century 21, the products offshoot of 'Thunderbirds'. Shackleton not only introduced a sister comic, *Lady Penelope*, after the success of 'Thunderbirds', but also the Rosenthal range of Thunderbirds toys at Harrogate Toy Fair in 1965. His subsequent sales drives took him to both the United States and Hong Kong. Shackleton, having travelled yet another century through time, now heads Century 22 Merchandising which is partially responsible for the current popularity of world wrestling.

Merchandising products include annuals, puppets and dolls, models of the Thunderbirds craft, dressing-up costumes and Lady Penelope accessories such as the hairband and, a real collector's item, the charm bracelet.

These souvenirs of an era are treasured and exhibited. There are dedicated collectors of Thunderbirds memorabilia as well as those who keep their single items in pride of place as a reminder of their favourite childhood series. With the revival of the Thunderbirds series, the associated publishing comes full circle. The first issue, in October 1991, of *Thunderbirds – the Comic* sold exceptionally well and the circulation continued to rise steadily with each issue.

Until the juggernaut-style merchandising campaigns of *Star Wars* and *Batman: The Movie*, no film or television merchandising operation had been as colossal or as successful as 'Thunderbirds'. With a new series of products recently launched, and likely to sell out rapidly, fans can also enjoy the recent Dire Straits video, *Calling Elvis*, to which collector-turned-modelmaker Philip Rae lent his assistance. Also involving the full participation of Gerry himself, it features 'Thunderbirds'-style puppet versions of band members whose bodies, along with those of certain 'Thunderbirds' characters who also appear, were based on Philip's Alan Tracy master-body. Philip also supplied the studio with photographs which enabled the re-creation of 'Thunderbirds' sets.

Fanderson, the official Gerry Anderson appreciation society, cannot be recommended highly enough to enthusiasts of all Gerry's series. A packed magazine, access to exclusive merchandising and a pen-pals' list, not to mention conventions which are attended by the series' creators, only require an annual subscription of £11 (Britain), £13 (Europe), £15 (America and Canada) or £17 (Australia and New Zealand). As well-motivated and big-hearted as Jeff himself, Fanderson is a non-profit-making organisation which gives generously to many different charities, including International Rescue Corps. Further details can be obtained by sending a stamped addressed envelope to:

Fanderson,
PO Box 93,
Wakefield,
West Yorkshire
WF1 1XJ

And thus 'Thunderbirds', a series which helped fuel the baby-boomers' reaction to postwar austerity, still enchants millions with its quirky fusion of supercharged spacecraft, cliffhanging feats of adventure and bobbing puppets, while paradoxically wrapping its reassuring emotional truths in a fetching air of magic. It will never be forgotten.

Thunderbirds – the Comic – the first issue. Within weeks of release Issue No. 1 has become a rare collectors' item – an excellent example of the continuing popularity of Thunderbirds merchandise.

INTERNATIONAL RESCUE CALLING

THUNDERBIRDS

65p

™

THE COMIC

October 19th - November 1st 1991   No.1

© 1991 ITC
Entertainment
Group Ltd

FREE THUNDERBIRDS ARE GO! BADGE

3

GREAT THUNDERBIRDS ADVENTURES IN GLORIOUS COLOUR

INSIDE

4 PAGE PULL-OUT WALL-CHART FEATURING TB1

ISSN 0963-9047

SUPER COMPETITION THUNDERBIRDS T-SHIRTS TO BE WON

INDEX